Harvard Business Review Guides

Arm yourself with the advice you need to succeed on the job, from the most trusted brand in business. Packed with how-to essentials from leading experts, the HBR Guides provide smart answers to your most pressing work challenges.

The titles include:

HBR Guide for Women at Work

HBR Guide to AI Basics for Managers

HBR Guide to Being a Great Boss

HBR Guide to Being More Productive

HBR Guide to Better Business Writing

HBR Guide to Better Mental Health at Work

HBR Guide to Building Your Business Case

HBR Guide to Buying a Small Business

HBR Guide to Changing Your Career

HBR Guide to Coaching Employees

HBR Guide to Collaborative Teams

HBR Guide to Critical Thinking

HBR Guide to Data Analytics Basics for Managers

HBR Guide to Dealing with Conflict

HBR Guide to Delivering Effective Feedback

HBR Guide to
Generative AI for Managers

Elisa Farri and
Gabriele Rosani

Capgemini

HARVARD BUSINESS REVIEW PRESS

Boston, Massachusetts

Copyright 2025 Harvard Business School Publishing Corporation

Printed in the United States of America

10 9 8 7 6 5 4 3 2

The web addresses referenced in this book were live and correct at the time of the book's publication but may be subject to change.

Library of Congress Cataloging-in-Publication data is forthcoming.

ISBN: 979-8-89279-047-5
eISBN: 979-8-89279-048-2

The paper used in this publication meets the requirements of the American National Standard for Permanence of Paper for Publications and Documents in Libraries and Archives Z39.48-1992.

HBR Guide to
Generative AI for Managers

This book is dedicated to the memory of Alessandro Di Fiore, whose insights and mentorship continue to inspire.

What You'll Learn

Generative artificial intelligence (gen AI) is transforming how organizations work, yet its profound impact on management is often overlooked. It is more than just an everyday productivity tool for drafting emails, summarizing long documents, and recording meeting minutes. In fact, gen AI can become a Co-Thinker for managers in organizations of all sizes, aiding in problem-solving and decision-making. It can become a sparring partner, providing fresh perspectives, challenging assumptions, and even enhancing strategic thinking and leadership development.

You can't afford to ignore how gen AI will enhance and transform your managerial role. If you don't understand how to work with gen AI, you risk missing out on its full benefits. And if you don't take personal action and develop new skills in this area, you risk a major career misstep.

Whether you want to get up to speed quickly, expand your knowledge, or experiment with gen AI for the first time, the *HBR Guide to Generative AI for Managers* will give you the information and skills you need. With practical, applicable advice and plain-language take-aways in each chapter, the book will help you unlock gen AI's full potential and prepare for the future.

You'll learn how to:

- Understand how machines are evolving into collaborators

- Explore the key terms and concepts that are shaping the future of management in the age of gen AI

- Envision how gen AI will enhance your job as manager

- Identify the right approaches for applying gen AI to your tasks

- Understand the potential traps and risks to consider when using gen AI

- Cultivate the right mindset to thrive in the gen AI–enabled workplace

- Interact practically with gen AI in two distinct modes: Co-Pilot and Co-Thinker

- Understand and practice how gen AI can support your individual tasks, from personal productivity to professional growth

- Leverage gen AI to help you better lead and support your team

- Engage in meaningful dialogues with gen AI to enhance your business decisions

- Use gen AI to help support organizational change

Contents

Contents

Contents

Introduction

Today, every leader and manager recognizes the efficiency and productivity benefits that generative AI brings to organizations across industries. But the benefits for individual managers can be less clear.

A survey of 1,100 leaders (director level and above) across 14 countries, conducted by the Capgemini Research Institute, revealed that generative AI is on the boardroom agenda in 95% of organizations, making it the fastest new technology to gain such high-level interest. Within these organizations, more than half (54%) of executives say their leadership is a strong advocate for gen AI. This number rises to 65% in the high-tech sector.[1]

However, according to our experience, and further confirmed in another survey of 1,400 managers, only 15% use gen AI at least once a day in their work.[2]

Clearly, a new knowing-doing gap has emerged around generative AI. Only those leaders who close it will reap its full benefits and thrive in the future.

WHAT IS GENERATIVE AI?

Generative AI (gen AI) is a type of artificial intelligence that can learn from and mimic large amounts of data to create content such as text, images, music, videos, code, and more, based on inputs or prompts.[a]

a. Harvard University Information Technology, https://huit.harvard.edu/ai#.

Fortunately, managers can close the gap quickly. Gen AI requires no coding skills. Gone are the days when data scientists, developers, and IT experts were the gatekeepers of AI. Today, anyone can interact with gen AI's natural language interface for their work.

Many factors may slow managers down as they integrate gen AI into their daily routines. Some managers assume that their individual role will not undergo significant change. Many are not aware of the diverse range of managerial tasks gen AI can assist them with. Others use it but don't know how to fully incorporate it into their regular workflows. In the absence of practical advice, tips, and a critical mass of hands-on experience, many managers hit a wall. They give up after a few attempts, fixate on mistakes or risks, or worst of all, they delegate its use to others and fall behind.

Whether you are new to management or a seasoned veteran, your success depends on your ability to use gen AI to do things differently. You cannot outsource or delegate it—it is *your* job and your imperative. You need to get your hands dirty with gen AI and understand how to use it for yourself, your team, and your business.

It's also your job to understand the challenges of generative AI. Along with its benefits, gen AI presents ethical, legal, security, and regulatory risks. As a manager, your responsibility is to set an example and shed light on the potential risks your team needs to consider.

What This Book Will Do for You

The *HBR Guide to Generative AI for Managers* will show you how to move past merely acknowledging the power of gen AI to actively using it in your daily work.

Drawing on the authors' expertise, this book offers practical tips, pitfalls to watch out for, and straightforward instructions derived from research, interviews with pioneers, and experiments.[3] It will guide you in applying novel concepts and tools to your work, with hands-on advice, templates, and examples for an immersive learning experience. Each chapter concludes with a summary of key points to help you put the ideas into practice.

The book blends knowledge acquisition with skill-building through practice. It is organized into five sections that begin by addressing gen AI's fundamental shift in how managers and machines work together, and the mindset you need to develop to work effectively and responsibly with gen AI. The book then moves through gen-AI-enhanced tasks for managing yourself, your team, and your business. Finally, the last section focuses on managing the complexity of organizational change with gen AI.

If you're new to gen AI concepts, we recommend reading the book straight through. If you already have a good understanding of the basics, we recommend reading section one (chapters 1–4) to familiarize yourself with a few key terms and approaches we will use throughout the book. Then take a look at the contents page, jump to any chapter, and start experimenting. If you run across any terms you are unfamiliar with, consult the glossary at the end of the book for helpful definitions of gen AI terms.

Most importantly, remember that this isn't just a book to read—it's a universal manual to get better results with *any* gen AI tool. As you flip through, you will often feel inspired to try something new with generative AI. Do it! Feel free to put this book down and try it right away. Expect ideas and inspiration to strike you frequently.

With this book, we hope you'll confidently position yourself at the forefront of the generative AI revolution. Rather than relying on others to explain what this technology can do, you'll discover its potential firsthand and integrate it into your everyday managerial responsibilities. This is your opportunity to be among the first pioneers to truly unlock the full potential of generative AI, to set a pace rather than play catch-up. And it's a chance to be a role model for the use of gen AI, inspiring your team, colleagues, and peers to follow in your footsteps.

NOTES

1. Capgemini Research Institute, Generative AI in Organizations survey, May–June 2024.

2. Capgemini Research Institute, Generative AI in Management survey, June–July 2024.

3. ManagementGPT, a joint experiment by Thinkers50 and Capgemini Invent, 2024, https://www.capgemini.com/insights/research-library/managementgpt-prototypes-of-ai-co-thinkers/.

Generative AI-Enabled Management

The Essentials

CHAPTER 1

Machines Are Evolving from Tools into Collaborators

While in the past machines were best seen as tools, today they are becoming collaborators. With the advent of generative AI models, managers can talk with machines in natural language, asking them to collaborate on tasks and engage in conversations. This chapter gives you a quick and essential refresher on that evolution.

The Old Paradigm: Machines as Tools

Throughout history, machines have transformed the way managers work. Personal computers automated and streamlined data processing. Emails revolutionized the way managers communicated with their teams. The emergence of search engines provided instant access to vast amounts of information, changing the landscape of research and decision-making. Smartphones have further evolved this dynamic, offering unprecedented connectivity and flexibility. Videoconferencing tools have introduced a new dimension of remote and hybrid work management.

Despite the transformative impact of technology on work, one fundamental aspect has endured: the mindset that technology and machines are tools. While increasingly powerful and sophisticated, machines have always been viewed fundamentally as enablers and executors. They have played a crucial role in automating repetitive tasks, analyzing vast amounts of data, and facilitating communication.

The realms of creativity and strategic thinking, however, have remained outside the scope of machines. Innovation and progress consistently originated from human collaboration and creativity. Innovation occurred most effectively when individuals worked together and built upon each other's ideas. Machines, no matter how advanced, were tools to be used, not partners to collaborate with. No manager would plausibly consider their laptop or email system as a collaborator. Firmly anchored in the concept of "tool," these technologies have played a marginal role in the human-led strategy and, at best, slightly aided in decision-making.

The Transitional Paradigm: Machines as Assistants

The introduction of AI systems sparked discussions about the most effective ways to integrate new technology with human efforts within organizations.[1] Managers assigned certain tasks to intelligent machines, leveraging their efficiency and analytical power, while other tasks, requiring human insight and creativity, remained under the managers' purview. However, the relationship between humans and machines was clearly distinct, with dual and complementary roles rather than a fusion. Although machines were becoming more intelligent, they were not yet ready to become collaborative partners.

In the 2010s, the way humans interacted with machines began to change with the introduction of AI virtual assistants. Gradually, machines started to engage with humans in natural language for simple requests.

Virtual assistants using natural language processing, such as Apple's Siri (launched in 2011), Microsoft's Cortana and Amazon's Alexa (both launched in 2014), or Google's Assistant (launched in 2016), demonstrated the ability to interact with humans. However, these versions of AI assistants had limitations. Their ability to understand and process human language was still developing, resulting in interactions that often felt robotic and restricted. Users often experienced frustration due to miscommunication or the inability of these systems to fully understand nuanced requests. As a result, AI virtual assistants were perceived more as gadgets and toys lacking the depth and adaptability for humanlike collaboration. Looking back on that era, in an interview with the *Financial Times*, Microsoft CEO Satya Nadella described the first wave of voice assistants as "dumb as a rock."[2]

Meanwhile, since the 2010s, various technologies have emerged. A notable example is the transformer architecture in the field of large language models (LLMs), which

WHAT ARE LARGE LANGUAGE MODELS?

A large language model is a text-generating AI foundation model trained to understand, generate, summarize, and translate human language and textual data. OpenAI's generative pre-trained transformer (GPT) is one example of an advanced LLM. (OpenAI's popular and well-known app ChatGPT provides an interface that allows users to access this LLM.)

Over time, LLMs have expanded their ability to deal with different modalities of inputs and outputs, for example, images and audio. Initially designed as a text-generating model, for instance, ChatGPT rolled out new voice and image capabilities, allowing it to see, hear, and speak with users.[a]

a. OpenAI, "ChatGPT Can Now See, Hear, and Speak," September 25, 2023, https://openai.com/index/chatgpt-can-now-see-hear-and-speak.

significantly enhanced the way machines understand and generate human language.[3] This leap forward has expanded the horizons of what machines can accomplish and paved the way for a new generation of AI virtual assistants capable of engaging in a seamless human-AI dialogue.

The Generative AI Paradigm: Machines as Collaborators

The release of OpenAI's ChatGPT to the general public in November 2022 marked a turning point in a new era of human-AI collaboration.[4] In the past, communicating with AI assistants did not resemble a conversation with a human being. With a conversational interface, ChatGPT enables much easier, more fluid, and more humanlike conversations.[5]

This changed the game. Suddenly, everyone was a programmer, even if they did not have any coding skill. The novelty of technologies like ChatGPT lies in their ability to provide authentic and conversational experiences in plain language. They can understand and generate content in a way that closely resembles human speech patterns, allowing them to respond to user input with great fluidity and sophistication. This simplicity led to rapid adoption—in just two months after its launch, OpenAI's ChatGPT reached 100 million monthly active users.[6] By comparison, it took TikTok about nine months after its global launch to reach 100 million users and Instagram two-and-a-half years, according to data from Sensor Tower.[7]

Unlike the first virtual assistants, which were constrained by predetermined responses, ChatGPT and other models like it are flexible and adaptable, capable of handling a wide range of questions, topics, and formats (text, image, audio, code, and so on). Their ability to maintain context across multiple conversations and respond to follow-up questions further enhances the user experience.

Generative AI can now help any manager with a wide range of tasks. While humans will always perform some managerial tasks, and machines will fully automate

DIFFERENT GEN AI MODELS ARE AVAILABLE

- *Generic public large language models* such as OpenAI's ChatGPT, Google's Gemini, Anthropic's Claude, Mistral's LeChat, and Meta's LLAMA2. These models are suited for a broad range of applications.

- *Specific public gen AI models* for specific applications such as Perplexity.ai for search, Adobe Firefly for image generation, and OpenAI's Sora or Google's Veo for video generation.

- *Custom gen AI models* for specific business needs. These models are tuned and trained on the company's data and proprietary knowledge.

- *Models integrated into software suites* such as Microsoft Copilot in Microsoft 365 and Google Gemini in Google Workspace.

Remember, the choice of the gen AI technology should always abide by the company's legal, ethics, cybersecurity, and data policies.

others, most managerial activities will exist in a blended interaction between humans and machines. This is a profound transformation; managers have never had this kind of symbiotic collaboration with technology.[8] It's no longer AI on one side, and human on the other. This new form of collaboration has immediate implications for the way managers do their tasks and longer-term implications for the way workflows are designed and organizations are structured.

The next chapter will explore the two collaborative modes you must understand: **Co-Pilot** for executing tasks with gen AI and **Co-Thinker** for engaging in constructive dialogue with gen AI.

RECAP

Throughout history, machines have transformed the way managers work, in the following ways:

- Traditionally, managers have viewed machines as tools rather than humanlike collaborators or thought partners.

- The traditional view started to change with the first virtual assistants, although the conversational capabilities of these AI systems were rather limited.

- With the advent of generative AI, machines are no longer just tools—they are collaborators we can talk to and ask to perform a broad range of tasks.

- Managers must learn how to ask gen AI to perform a task and to engage in humanlike dialogue.

NOTES

1. H. James Wilson and Paul R. Daugherty, "Collaborative Intelligence: Humans and AI Are Joining Forces," *Harvard Business Review*, July–August 2018, https://hbr.org/2018/07/collaborative-intelligence-humans-and-ai-are-joining-forces.

2. Dave Lee, "Amazon's Big Dreams for Alexa Fall Short," *Financial Times*, March 6, 2023, https://www.ft.com/content/bab905bd-a2fa-4022-b63d-a385c2a0fb86.

3. Ashish Vaswani et al., "Attention Is All You Need," 31st Conference on Neural Information Processing Systems, 2017.

4. Ethan Mollick, "ChatGPT Is a Tipping Point for AI," hbr.org, December 14, 2023, https://hbr.org/2022/12/chatgpt-is-a-tipping-point-for-ai.

5. Jaime Teevan, "To Work Well with GenAI, You Need to Learn How to Talk to It," hbr.org, December 15, 2023, https://hbr.org/2023/12/to-work-well-with-genai-you-need-to-learn-how-to-talk-to-it.

6. Krystal Hu, "ChatGPT Sets Record for Fastest-Growing User Base," Reuters, February 2, 2023, https://www.reuters.com/technology/chatgpt-sets-record-fastest-growing-user-base-analyst-note-2023-02-01/.

7. Hu, "ChatGPT Sets Record for Fastest-Growing User Base."

8. Paul Baier, David DeLallo, and John J. Sviokla, "Your Organization Isn't Designed to Work with GenAI," hbr.org, February 26, 2024, https://hbr.org/2024/02/your-organization-isnt-designed-to-work-with-genai.

CHAPTER 2

Generative AI as a Co-Pilot and Co-Thinker

Managers can collaborate with generative AI through two primary modes: *Co-Pilot* and *Co-Thinker*.

When used as a *Co-Pilot*, gen AI becomes the manager's efficient collaborator, handling a wide range of administrative, communication, and operational tasks. Tasks that are better suited for Co-Pilot interaction are those where the manager's main contribution is the initial direction, final review, and validation of the output.

When used as a *Co-Thinker*, gen AI becomes the manager's thought partner, engaging in conversation, suggesting new perspectives, and challenging assumptions or ideas. Tasks that are better suited for a Co-Thinker interaction require methodological guidance and structured reflection (such as weighing options, assessing risks, or considering different points of view).

How to Use Gen AI as a Co-Pilot

When using gen AI as a Co-Pilot, your focus is on execution and productivity.

To start, you need to ask gen AI to perform a task for you—the instruction that you give is called a *prompt*. Prompts are how you craft the input, such as "Transform this FAQ list into a 10-slide presentation," "Summarize the meeting's action items," or "Write three paragraphs about our company's sustainability strategy." Prompting is about providing clear instructions and relevant context, just as you would do with a human collaborator. Gen AI completes the task as instructed, then you check and validate.

HOW TO PROMPT GEN AI TO EXECUTE A TASK FOR YOU

The way in which you *prompt* gen AI to perform a task impacts the quality of the output it produces. When creating a prompt, act as if you were talking to a human collaborator who needs the right context and instructions to do a task well.

Be precise and contextual. Vague prompts like "Write an email" produce generic results and inaccurate responses. Always make sure you write accurate sentences. Add contextual details first, and then ask gen

AI to comment or answer your question.[a] By providing enough background information, clear goals, as well as a list of the information sources gen AI should use, performance will improve.

Specify the format of the output. Gen AI can handle different types of outputs, including code, text, audio, images, and videos. After giving clear instructions, specify your preferred output format, such as "Produce a [*specify, for example, a table, list, paragraph, image*] about [*specify topic*] that contains . . . [*add details*]." This will give the gen AI a reference point.

Give examples. Providing gen AI with examples is crucial for improving its performance. The "few shots" technique is a good example of how you can give a few specific examples, typically between two and five, to help AI better understand the task and replicate the desired output.[b]

Set boundaries. Telling gen AI the scope of the work can save time and improve your result. If you need assistance in creating a market trend report, specifying your criteria will yield more targeted results. For instance, instead of requesting an overview of the main trends in the Asian renewable energy market, you could specify focusing solely on solar and wind energy in a particular country, such as China. This will enable gen AI to provide a more customized and precise analysis.

(Continued)

Ask gen AI for help. When you get stuck or simply don't know how to request gen AI to perform a task, simply ask, "I want to [*specify*]; how can you help me?" or "Give me three prompts I can use to [*specify*]." Generative AI is well versed in transforming your intentions into detailed prompts.

a. Pranab Islam et al., "FinanceBench: A New Benchmark for Financial Question Answering," Cornell University working paper, November 20, 2023, https://arxiv.org/abs/2311.11944.

b. Tom B. Brown et al., "Language Models Are Few-Shot Learners," Cornell University working paper, May 28, 2020, https://arxiv.org/abs/2005.14165.

As generative AI capabilities are increasingly built into the software products you are likely to use every day (such as Microsoft 365 Copilot for Office and Google Gemini for Workspace), gen AI as a Co-Pilot can execute a wider range of tasks. Often these tasks only require a single click on a ready-to-use prompt, suggested by gen AI automatically. Here are a few examples:

- In Microsoft Word or Google Docs, you can ask gen AI to draft and edit text or extract key information from long documents.

- In Microsoft PowerPoint or Google Slides, you can ask gen AI to turn documents into slideshows, create new presentations from existing notes or from scratch, and add new content or slides.

- In Microsoft Excel or Google Sheets, you can ask gen AI to clean a spreadsheet, analyze a database, and generate formulas.

- In Microsoft Outlook or Google Gmail, you can ask gen AI to find information quickly in your inbox, draft messages, and summarize threads.

- In Microsoft Teams or Google Meet, you can ask gen AI to take notes; contribute to the discussion with ideas, information, or data; and summarize the meeting.

While gen AI can perform an increasing number of tasks, don't confuse Co-Pilot with an autopilot. You should always be in the loop to verify the output before proceeding. Over-relying on gen AI's first drafts can result in mistakes and other significant risks. The AI-generated content may lack the necessary quality, accuracy, or trustworthiness required in a business environment. For example, it may create from scratch a citation or a source, known as "fabrications," or outputs that are confident sounding but factually incorrect, known as "hallucinations." It is imperative that you abide by your company's legal, ethics, cybersecurity, and data policies, and always use your judgment about the output.

How to Use Gen AI as a Co-Thinker

When using gen AI as a Co-Thinker, your focus is on strategic thinking and problem-solving through human-machine conversation.

As a Co-Thinker, you will engage with the AI in a deep, reflective dialogue. This can help you solve problems, become a better leader, or brainstorm innovative concepts.[1]

Begin by thinking of a conversation you'd like to have with a real person and building a sequence of questions and topics you want to explore. For example, consider asking gen AI to act as one of your clients with whom you are having an important meeting in a few days. Based on the context and details that you provide, gen AI can simulate potential client questions, challenge your presentation, or push you out of your comfort zone. Or perhaps ask gen AI to help you and your team unearth the root causes of a problem by providing methodological guidance and then debating the pros and cons of potential solutions with you.

Co-Thinking represents a process done together, as the "co" implies, where human and AI intertwine. It goes far beyond simple Q&A or pushing a button and getting an output. It involves an active back-and-forth process where both the human and the AI contribute ideas and build upon each other's inputs, at every step of the dialogue (see table 2-1).

TABLE 2-1

Roles of AI and humans in collaborative dialogue

What AI brings to the dialogue	What the human brings to the dialogue
Articulate, exemplify, give options, wear different hats, propose, elaborate, recommend, analyze pros and cons, give different perspectives, challenge opinions . . .	Provide context, give input, define criteria, provide feedback, comment, add or drop options or ideas, choose, select, validate, make the final decision . . .

FIGURE 2-1

Four steps to prepare for a Co-Thinking dialogue

1. Assign a role to AI	2. Define the setting	3. Outline the dialogue	4. Create the prompt
Act as . . . Help me . . . The output of the dialogue will be . . .	Define who is taking part in the conversation One-on-one or one-to-many	Clarify sequence of dialogue What AI brings What the human brings	Translate the flow into a full text prompt

To successfully engage gen AI as a Co-Thinker, you will need to give instructions for the type of dialogue you want to have and the role the AI should play. Providing a clear structure and flow is essential to keep the dialogue focused and productive, especially when the content is complex. There are four steps you must take to prepare for a Co-Thinking dialogue with gen AI:

1. Assign a role.

2. Define the setting.

3. Outline the dialogue.

4. Create the prompt.

Let's explore each in turn.

Assign a role

Depending on the topic you want to discuss, you can ask gen AI to assume a specific role such as a teammate, a mentor, or a devil's advocate. This step goes beyond simply telling gen AI to act as an expert or coach. You need to describe the profile in detail, the context it needs to immerse itself in, and the approach or methodology it should follow during the conversation.

Defining the role the AI will play involves articulating a clear identity based on the objectives and desired outcome. The machine is highly versatile and can fulfill various roles. For instance, these roles could range from serving as a virtual workshop facilitator to acting as an expert in sustainability. This can also benefit the manager, who can better envision a humanlike conversation by imagining AI as a knowledgeable partner. This fosters a switch in mindset, where the human sees the AI not just as a tool but as a collaborator.

Define the setting

The dialogue with gen AI as a Co-Thinker does not have to be limited to the conventional setting with a manager sitting at a desk facing a laptop or mobile screen and interacting with AI. For example, engaging in a one-on-one dialogue with gen AI can provide input and foster self-reflection. Gen AI can go beyond a one-on-one thought partner. It can also be involved in one-to-many conversations with managers and their teams.

EXPLORING THE SETTINGS OF CO-THINKING

One-to-one. In this typical setting, you interact directly with a gen AI model. It's a private environment, ideal for individual tasks, self-reflection, or learning.

One-to-many. In a workshop setting, a gen AI model interacts with a group of people. It can play various roles: facilitator of the discussion, team member generating ideas, or expert steering the conversation by providing specialized knowledge.

Many-to-many. This more complex setting involves multiple gen AI models interacting with a group of people, for instance, in a collaboration, where ideas and feedback are exchanged among AI and humans.

Many-to-one. In this setting, you interact with more than one gen AI model, each specialized in different roles or a specific task. You can also use this setting to compare the performance of two gen AI models.

Outline the dialogue

Using gen AI as a Co-Thinker hinges on a well-thought-out flow of exchanges and a harmonious complement of parties. It ensures that your strengths, knowledge, and unique insights are effectively intertwined and leveraged with AI. Leaving the flow of the dialogue to chance risks it will go offtrack and create limited value.

To have a successful Co-Thinking dialogue, you must outline a script for your gen AI. In Co-Thinking, humans and machines play different roles, creating a dialogue. To outline your dialogue, begin by clarifying your intention and envisioning a sequence of questions and statements. Follow these four principles to outline your dialogue successfully:

- **Define a well-balanced sequence.** Memorable conversations are characterized by good content and emotional engagement. The same is true for using gen AI as a Co-Thinker. While the flow of the dialogue needs clear steps and instructions, it should also include elements that spur reflection, articulation, and elaboration. Too much structure can dampen emotional engagement, but too little can lead to distractions and off-topic detours.

- **Delineate the conversation.** Define rules and boundaries for gen AI to follow during conversations. Consider adding content guardrails to ensure gen AI stays on topic and uses correct information sources. Use process guardrails to control how gen AI follows the predefined sequence, such as "In each of the steps, please wait for my feedback before proceeding to the next step."

- **Take different perspectives.** Generative AI is very good at taking on different roles and providing different perspectives. It can draw parallels to analogous situations or generate insights. During the conversation, you can leverage this ability for richer exploration of topics, considering the perspectives of different stakeholders you may have overlooked.

- **Encourage active participation.** Gen AI should encourage you to better articulate your input and answers, not reduce it to a simple yes or no or

"OK, I agree." Instruct the machine to ask for your feedback and concrete examples in your specific context, based on your own experience.

EXAMPLE OF A DIALOGUE OUTLINE
Q&A Session Preparation

Consider the case of a manager preparing to handle the Q&A session of an important presentation.

[*Step 1*] Gen AI asks the manager to provide contextual input about the topic, main messages, and the audience for the upcoming Q&A session.

[*Step 2*] Gen AI generates a list of 10 potential tough questions the audience might ask. The manager provides feedback and selects three questions that are the most challenging to handle.

[*Step 3*] Gen AI suggests responses to each selected question. The manager reviews these responses to ensure they align with the company's messaging.

[*Step 4*] Gen AI engages the manager in a dialogue that simulates the Q&A session to help the manager practice delivering responses and handling follow-up questions.

If you get stuck when outlining the dialogue, remember to ask gen AI to help you. For example, try this: "Please create a structured outline for a step-by-step dialogue about [*specify the topic*] with the goal of [*specify*]. For each step, clarify my role and yours."

Create the prompt

The outline is a preparatory step to the prompt (the actual text instruction to type or copy into the input box of the gen AI model). Once the outline is ready, you can translate it into a clear, structured prompt that AI can understand and execute. If you are new to working with generative AI or translating your ideas into prompts, don't worry. You can ask gen AI to help you with this. For example, "I have this outline of a dialogue and need your help turning it into a structured prompt that you can run with me: '[*insert your outline here*].'" Throughout this book, in most chapters that explore Co-Thinking tasks, you will find URLs related to specific dialogue prompts that you can easily copy and paste into your gen AI model.

Remember, there's no single right way to interact with generative AI. Fine-tune your prompts if the results don't meet your expectations. And if you're ever in doubt or want to explore different prompts, don't hesitate to seek AI's assistance. The machine is very skilled at structured, advanced prompting and can also suggest how to improve your own prompt.[2]

This has been a brief overview of the concept of Co-Thinking and a preview of the process of outlining dialogues for successful Co-Thinking. Throughout sections two to five of the book, you'll find many ideas to spur your human-machine conversations, spanning many aspects of managerial work, from personal growth to leading your team.

ADVANCED TECHNIQUE FOR STRUCTURED PROMPTING

When you want human-machine dialogue to tackle a complex topic, it's often helpful to break the prompt into step-by-step instructions. The "chain of thought"[a] technique helps you instruct gen AI to go through the process one step at a time, rather than jumping to the final answer ("Go step by step"). The prompt should clearly highlight the different steps ("First do this . . . Then do that . . . "). In order to have a thoughtful conversation with gen AI, specify where and how you will contribute ("Wait for my comments after step [*specify*]" or "Solicit my feedback before moving to the next step").

a. Jason Wei et al., "Chain-of-Thought Prompting Elicits Reasoning in Large Language Models," Cornell University working paper, January 28, 2022, https://arxiv.org/abs/2201.11903.

Key Differences Between Co-Pilot and Co-Thinker

The way you interact with gen AI as a Co-Thinker differs significantly from that as a Co-Pilot in three dimensions:[3]

1. **A Co-Pilot *answers* questions, while a Co-Thinker *engages in dialogue with you.*** When you use gen AI in a collaborative thinking process, the machine can operate similarly to the Socratic

method, enhancing your critical thinking through dialogue. Questions are typically open-ended, prompting further discussion. For instance, gen AI can act as a methodology expert that suggests the appropriate questions to solve a complex problem, elaborates on your answers, introduces new ideas, and leads to follow-up questions.

2. **A Co-Pilot *executes for you*, while a Co-Thinker *collaborates with you*.** In the Co-Pilot mode, you provide clear instructions, such as "Please draft a follow-up message to this email" and wait for the task to be completed. It's a one-way street where you ask a question and the AI delivers an answer. On the other hand, in the Co-Thinker mode, you need to actively engage with the machine in a back-and-forth interaction. Ideas flow freely; both parties contribute with feedback and mutual challenges, and ultimately cocreate the output together.

3. **A Co-Pilot helps you go *quickly*, while a Co-Thinker helps you *pause and reflect*.** Speed is undoubtedly one of the key benefits of using gen AI as a Co-Pilot. However, when you need reflection, speed may backfire. That's why you should prompt gen AI for thoughtfulness over speed in Co-Thinker mode. Ask gen AI to ask you reflective questions, encourage you to take a pause and do activities conducive to deeper analysis (such as customer interviews), or restart the conversation with a fresh perspective after a break.

Finally, Co-Pilot and Co-Thinker are not mutually exclusive modes. They can be used separately or in sequence. For example, you might reflect on a problem-solving task (using gen AI as a Co-Thinker) and then produce a written memo of that conversation (using gen AI as a Co-Pilot). Conversely, when preparing for a meeting, you can start using gen AI as a Co-Pilot to draft the speaking notes from your presentation and then switch to a Co-Thinker mode, rehearsing with gen AI to simulate client questions and raise potential objections. In real scenarios, your tasks do not exist in a vacuum; they are linked in a chain as part of broader workflows. Therefore, depending on your workflow, some tasks may be suited for a Co-Pilot mode and others for a Co-Thinker.

Now that we have covered the basics of *how* to interact with generative AI, we move to the mindset you'll need to collaborate with the technology effectively and responsibly.

RECAP

Gen AI can assist with a variety of tasks through two primary modes of interaction: *Co-Pilot* and *Co-Thinker*.

- When used as a *Co-Pilot*, gen AI executes a task for you.

- When used as a *Co-Thinker*, gen AI becomes your thought partner, engaging in a dialogue.

NOTES

1. Hal Gregersen and Nicola Morini Bianzino, "AI Can Help You Ask Better Questions—and Solve Bigger Problems," hbr.org, May 26, 2023, https://hbr.org/2023/05/ai-can-help-you-ask-better-questions -and-solve-bigger-problems.

2. Oguz A. Acar, "AI Prompt Engineering Isn't the Future," hbr .org, June 6, 2023, https://hbr.org/2023/06/ai-prompt-engineering -isnt-the-future.

3. Elisa Farri and Gabriele Rosani, "Why Managers Need an AI Co-Thinker," *MIT Sloan Management Review Polska*, February 1, 2024, https://mitsmr.pl/a/dlaczego-menedzerowie-potrzebuja -wspolmysliciela-ai/D12kjzgaD.

CHAPTER 3

A New Mindset That Successful Managers Need to Master

As you begin to use gen AI in your daily work, you'll experience a mix of emotions, including excitement, curiosity, and perhaps even a touch of apprehension. At times, it may feel like you're embarking on a journey into the unknown, surrounded by uncertainty and anxiety around change. Don't worry, these feelings are perfectly normal. You have probably experienced them in past digital transformations. Your mindset lies at the center of every transformation and influences how you perceive, embrace, and adapt to change. Adopting the right mindset around generative AI will help you explore and experiment confidently and responsibly.

Building Blocks of Your Gen AI Mindset

Let's look at what is specific about the gen AI transformation and how it impacts your mindset as a manager:

- **Gen AI talks with you.** For the first time in history, you can have meaningful conversations with machines without having to code. You can communicate in simple, natural language (in dozens of languages spoken worldwide). Increasingly, voice-to-voice capabilities make the experience even easier and frictionless. This conversational aspect makes gen AI remarkably relatable and accessible. Using it feels more like speaking with a knowledgeable partner than interacting with a machine. What's more, the machine can take on a variety of different roles, as well as different tones of voice, with a humanlike touch. Based on the role you assign to gen AI, you must adjust your mindset accordingly. For instance, if you assign it the role of a business challenger, you must be prepared to build on the feedback, share examples and contextual details, and debate additional perspectives it suggests. The more contextual awareness, ethical reasoning, and judgment you bring to the conversation, the more high-quality gen AI's output will be.

- **Gen AI evolves quickly.** Gen AI refuses to stand still. It evolves and improves at a truly remarkable pace. Consider, for example, the significant progress made in only one year after OpenAI's ChatGPT was released: New models of gen AI chatbots were launched by other players, new features were added (mainly thanks to the integration of text, voice, images, and video), new offerings emerged (such as GPT stores for chatbots), as well as new AI products (such as AI agents). In this rapidly evolving environment, it is critical to stay abreast of the ever-expanding capabilities and applications of gen AI. You must be able to understand the fundamental changes and direction of evolution and to anticipate and interpret the trends. This involves a good amount of curiosity and reading, coupled with practical experimentation and hands-on experience to better understand the potential applications and current limitations of the technology.

- **Gen AI can "hallucinate."** Unlike tools such as calculators that always provide accurate results, gen AI models are based on statistical methods that don't always produce the same answers to identical queries. This makes gen AI occasionally prone to error or information fabrication. Using gen AI to its fullest while avoiding these pitfalls requires a fundamentally different mindset than you have with technology that is error-free. This risk underscores the importance of vigilance and the development of robust guardrails. When using gen AI, you should address unintended consequences, risks, and biases.

HOW TO STAY UP-TO-DATE ON THE LATEST TRENDS IN GEN AI

- Experiment with new AI models and functionalities.

- Encourage your team to experiment with generative AI in their tasks and then report back on learnings and challenges.

- Join gen-AI-related social media groups and professional networks. Engage in discussions, ask questions, and share insights with experts in the field.

- Actively contribute to internal communities and discuss new tools and emerging applications with community members.

- Follow the top AI experts and companies at the forefront of gen AI.

- Read the latest reports, including research papers. Consider opportunities to contribute to or collaborate on academic research projects.

- Attend webinars, listen to podcasts, or ask AI directly for the latest AI trends.

- Consider mentorship opportunities to learn from experienced professionals.

When getting started with gen AI, you may feel hindered by concerns about hallucinations, biased responses, misinformation, and other potential traps. Yet, it's crucial not to let apprehension impede exploration and experimentation. Only through firsthand experience can you gain insights into navigating its capabilities confidently and responsibly, ensuring its beneficial application for both you and your organization.

HUMAN-AI COLLABORATION TRAPS TO AVOID

Trust trap: *Overreliance on gen AI may lead to complacency.*

- In this trap, humans excessively trust gen AI output without exercising their critical judgment, driven by laziness or a superficial impression that AI's responses "sound good enough." This lack of active engagement and critical thinking can lead to mistakes, oversights, or misunderstandings.

- Users should actively probe AI's reasoning by asking for clarifications and better articulation, requesting counterarguments, and identifying weak points.

Fabrication trap: *Gen AI can fabricate facts and sources that you may accept as true.*

- In this trap, humans unquestionably accept gen AI output as factual without verifying it. Many

(Continued)

are not even aware of the risk of AI's fabrication. The authoritative tone of language models further fuels this risk.

- Users should validate statements against established facts from reputable sources and consult experts, particularly on unfamiliar topics.

Conformity trap: *Gen AI's ideas may limit diverse thinking if you are too deferential.*

- In this trap, humans don't tailor or customize AI's suggestions to their specific context and needs, resulting in generic output lacking diversity and originality.

- Users should actively provide AI with contextual information (for example, about your company's values, unique value proposition, brand, and so on) and ask AI to consider it as a guideline throughout the creative process. Also, users should encourage AI to push lateral thinking and avoid overly common ideas.

Speed trap: *Gen AI executes quickly; you tend to rush through without reflection.*

- In this trap, humans tend to type, click, or advance too hastily.

- Users should slow down, think critically, and actively participate in the conversation. They should articulate their own perspectives and counterarguments.

Solo trap: *Gen AI is used in an isolated way, rather than opening up the collaboration to the team.*

- In this trap, a human works predominantly alone with generative AI tools, rather than actively involving and engaging with their human teammates. This can reduce interpersonal communication and knowledge sharing within the team, resulting in more siloed work and a lack of diverse perspectives.

- Users should take breaks from solo AI interactions to engage face-to-face with teammates, involve other colleagues in the AI-aided process, seek feedback, integrate diverse viewpoints, and encourage peer learning.

Building Your Gen AI Mindset

These guidelines can help you as a manager navigate this transformative landscape with the right mindset:

- **Embrace a conversational approach.** Approaching gen AI as if you're talking to a human, rather than passively receiving information, helps it understand what you're asking for (for example, you need to provide clear instructions and contextual information for performing a task in the same way you would with a human collaborator). Having a conversational approach is even more important when you want to use gen AI as a thought partner. You can't expect appropriate advice, tailored answers, and suggestions if you don't follow up with additional questions, share your personal experience, and challenge AI's point of view. Remember that your brain may resist because gen AI is not a human, even though it gives you the impression that it is.

HOW TO MAKE IT CONVERSATIONAL

Be respectful. Use polite language and show gratitude with words like "please" and "thank you." Although gen AI does not have feelings or emotions, showing appreciation can have a positive impact on your mindset and keep your brain in a conversational mode.

Be flexible. Adapt your tone of voice and style to match the role you envision for gen AI. By mirroring the effective communication strategies used in human interactions, the conversation can become more humanlike.

Be clear. Just as you would with a human, ask clear questions and give complete instructions when communicating with gen AI. Take your time and formulate full sentences to ensure that the machine comprehends your input.

Be patient. You may not get the answer you want on the first try when using gen AI. In such cases, try re-phrasing or clarifying your question.

Be focused. Good conversations stay on topic and lead to a clear outcome. Avoid jumping across un-related topics. Once you feel that the discussion has reached a satisfactory conclusion, declare it and say goodbye and thank you.

Be motivating. Encouraging AI with specific prompts can help improve its performance. For instance, you may want to use phrases like "This is really important for my job," "This is crucial for my decision-making," or "You can do it. I believe in you."

Be proactive in getting help. Every time you think "I'm stuck" or "I don't know how to do this with gen AI," seek assistance from gen AI itself. For example, you can ask, "Could you please show me how to do [*specify*]?" or "I tried this prompt [*specify*] to [*specify the goal*], but it's not working well. Please help me improve it."

- **Test and share regularly.** With rapid tech ad-vances, trying different gen AI models is key to understanding what it can do for you, your team, and your business. You can't delegate this learning. Hands-on testing reveals capabilities, limitations, effective usage techniques, risks, and potential

mitigations. Adopting a learning mindset—asking
"What if?"—can help you reap the full benefits.
More importantly, instill this hands-on exploratory mindset in your team. Encourage them to
experiment firsthand and help others to use gen
AI. Explain the value of taking ownership of this
continuous learning process and foster an environment in which people share the innovative practices and learnings.[1]

TIP
Cultivating the Gen AI Habit

Thinking of gen AI first. Using gen AI models may not
come naturally at first. One effective reminder is to
place a sticky note on your laptop with questions like
"Have you asked the gen AI model?" or "Would the gen
AI model have performed this task differently?"

Encouraging your team. As a manager, spur your
team to use gen AI in addition to defaulting to traditional routines. Continuously asking, "Have you tried
using the chatbot?" can be a helpful way to promote
its use.

Embracing versatility. By experimenting with multiple models, you can identify the ones best suited to
your specific needs and tasks. Some models may excel
at summarizing long documents, while others may be
better at tasks like searching or creating marketing materials. Additionally, performance can vary depending

on the model (and for the same model, depending on which version you are using). Prompting techniques may differ across models, further emphasizing the importance of trying various approaches. That's why trying different things develops versatility rather than sticking to only one model or version. Moreover, you may find it useful to jump from model to model or to compare the output quality of different models for the same prompts.

- **Use it responsibly.** Using generative AI without safety measures and a responsible mindset is risky and potentially dangerous. While technology developers continuously work to improve gen AI by pretraining and tuning the large language models, the ultimate responsibility still rests with the users. This responsibility starts with you, as a leader, being aware of your company policies and local laws. It then extends to your team members, who need your support in understanding the policies and regulations, and ensuring that they are aware of the potential risks. Your role is to strike the right balance when discussing what can and can't be done, making sure you don't stifle your team's innovation potential. Use real-world simulations to make your team aware of the risks of gen AI, while promoting shared responsibility by making it clear that gen AI should augment human judgment, never replace it.

RISKS IN THE AGE OF GENERATIVE AI

Demonstrating ethical, risk-aware behavior is one of your primary duties as a manager. It is an obligation you have to your company and its shareholders, as well as to the people you manage. With the complexities at the intersection of ethics and generative AI, you must adhere to your company policy and raise your level of attention. Gen AI risks are real, and there are no quick fixes.

These are examples of risks you and your team should consider:

Privacy and data protection. Putting your own personal data or your company's proprietary information into a public generative AI model raises concerns about losing control of it. Such data could be used to further train the model and, potentially, reveal your data to other users.[a] Even seemingly anonymized data poses risks, as gen AI can remove the anonymity and reidentify individuals, undermining privacy protections.

Intellectual property infringement. Because current foundational gen AI models are often trained with massive amounts of publicly available data, they might faithfully regurgitate output with copyrighted data.

Bias and fairness. Gen AI models will reflect the biases present in their training data. This can lead to social discrimination (against certain population groups based on gender or ethnicity) or product biases.

Environmental sustainability. The resources required for initial training and operational use of gen AI models can have a significant carbon footprint if they rely on computationally intensive approaches. To address this challenge, there are various energy-conserving computational models to use when large models don't add significant value.[b]

a. Glenn Cohen, Theodoros Evgeniou, and Martin Husovec, "Navigating the New Risks and Regulatory Challenges of GenAI," hbr.org, November 20, 2023, https://hbr.org/2023/11/navigating-the-new-risks-and-regulatory-challenges-of-genai.

b. Ajay Kumar and Tom Davenport, "How to Make Generative AI Greener," hbr.org, July 20, 2023, https://hbr.org/2023/07/how-to-make-generative-ai-greener.

Armed with this new mindset about using generative AI, you are ready to start exploring how it can enhance your daily work—whether in the role of a Co-Pilot or a Co-Thinker. The next chapter will introduce a list of 35 common management tasks that can be enhanced with gen AI, each of which we will cover in detail throughout the book.

RECAP

To thrive in the age of generative AI, managers should adopt a new mindset that has three characteristics:

- Conversational: Actively engaging in structured dialogues with gen AI

- Experimental: Becoming familiar with gen AI through self-directed immersion—not passive consumption—to stay relevant in the future

- Responsible: Demonstrating moral behavior, prioritizing good judgment, and promoting risk-aware, ethical behavior on your team

NOTE

1. Maryam Alavi and George Westerman, "How Generative AI Will Transform Knowledge Work," hbr.org, November 7, 2023, https://hbr .org/2023/11/how-generative-ai-will-transform-knowledge-work.

CHAPTER 4

Thirty-Five Managerial Tasks That Can Be Enhanced with Generative AI

In the previous chapters, you learned that gen AI can serve as either a Co-Pilot or a Co-Thinker, depending on the nature of the task you are hoping to accomplish. You also learned about the key differences between these two modes of interaction with the machine, and how to adopt the right mindset for using and experimenting with generative AI.

With this foundation, the remainder of the book is devoted to 35 common management tasks that can be enhanced with generative AI (table 4-1). These groups are divided into four main categories that correspond with sections two to five of this book: managing yourself, managing your team, managing your business, and managing change. The 35 tasks are evenly split between using gen AI as a Co-Pilot and as a Co-Thinker.

The 35 tasks comprise a wide range of common items and responsibilities that every manager typically encounters in their job, but the list is not exhaustive. As the technology develops further, more uses will evolve. The tasks explored in this book are general rather than field-specific; no matter your role, you will be able to start experimenting today on tasks that apply to your job—from creative endeavors to technical work.

The book provides suggestions and examples to help you understand where gen AI creates value in your professional life. For each task, you can practice using gen AI, drawing inspiration from "Try this" tips or "Dialogue outlines." You can input these tips and prompts into your AI system or customize them to your specific needs and context. If your initial prompt doesn't yield the desired results, try rephrasing it and seeing if it triggers a better response. We will remind you again throughout the book that you can ask the gen AI system directly how best to phrase your prompt.

Now that you are through this first section, you can read this book chapter by chapter, or you can start with the tasks that are most relevant to your current priorities. As we have said, you should feel free at any time to put down the book, formulate a prompt, and see how gen AI can help you with your task. So, turn the page or flip ahead—it's time to start experimenting with generative AI.

TABLE 4-1

Thirty-five managerial tasks that can be enhanced with gen AI

	Co-Pilot	Co-Thinker
Section 2: Managing yourself	**Personal productivity** • Email management • Time management • Summarization **Content generation** • Text writing • Slide creation	**Personal growth** • Self-reflection on leadership styles • Soliciting feedback **Persuasive communication** • Speech preparation • Job interview preparation
Section 3: Managing teams	**Team operational support** • Meeting management • Goal setting and articulation • Task planning and reporting **Team creativity support** • Team composition • Idea generation	**Leading teams** • Crafting team purpose • Designing high-quality work • Facilitating conflict resolution **Complex problem-solving** • Problem framing • Root cause analysis • Problem storytelling
Section 4: Managing business	**Data analysis support** • Information search • Data analysis and visualization **Customer insights** • Research design and analysis • Synthetic research	**Business case development** • Stakeholder perspectives • Evaluating trade-offs • Risk identification and mitigation **Strategic decisions** • Formulating business strategy • Evaluating innovative concepts • Assessing supply chain strategy
Section 5: Managing change	**Transformation support** • Planning and monitoring • Communication and engagement	**Leading change** • Defining the transformation strategy • Overcoming resistance • Promoting a mindset shift

Managing Yourself with Generative AI

CHAPTER 5

Self-Management Tasks That Are Enhanced with Gen AI

In your day-to-day job as a manager, there are many different tasks that you juggle as an individual contributor. Sometimes it can feel as if your responsibilities are pulling you in a hundred different directions at once. Applying generative AI to these tasks can help you get organized and work more efficiently. As you become more productive, you will have more time and energy to focus on yourself, both personally and professionally, and ultimately become a better leader.

When used as a Co-Pilot, gen AI for managing yourself can help you improve your personal productivity.

TABLE 5-1

Self-management tasks enhanced with gen AI

	Co-Pilot	Co-Thinker
Managing yourself	**Personal productivity** • Email management • Time management • Summarization **Content generation** • Text writing • Slide creation	**Personal growth** • Self-reflection on leadership styles • Soliciting feedback **Persuasive communication** • Speech preparation • Job interview preparation

Examples range from managing your time (notably your calendar), sorting and drafting emails, summarizing long documents, to producing content (including text, images, video, or audio). For tasks that fall into this category, your effort as a manager consists of providing input, refining, and validating the output. Consider the example of taking meeting minutes: Gen AI as a Co-Pilot produces a first draft, which you should always review to ensure it accurately captures all action items and next steps. Typically, the main benefit of using gen AI as a Co-Pilot for these tasks is speed.

When used as a Co-Thinker, gen AI for managing yourself becomes your thought partner. For personal growth, it guides you through deep reflection on your leadership styles and behaviors, as well as on how to solicit feedback for continuous self-improvement. For professional growth, it helps you become an effective communicator, from speech to job interview preparation. In general, the benefits of using gen AI as a Co-Thinker for these tasks are twofold: methodological guidance and structured reflection.

There are also tasks that may require switching between the two modes to complete successfully: You can leverage gen AI as a Co-Thinker to help you craft a compelling speech, and then when you are satisfied with the main storytelling and messages, use gen AI as a Co-Pilot to produce the slide deck that supports your speech. Conversely, you might draft a cover letter using gen AI as a Co-Pilot and then, as a Co-Thinker, simulate potential interview questions based on your résumé and cover letter.

In the first part of this section, you will learn how to practice gen AI as a Co-Pilot for personal productivity (chapter 6) and for content generation (chapter 7) with concrete examples of prompts that you can try. In the second part of this section, you will learn how to practice gen AI as a Co-Thinker for personal growth (chapter 8) and persuasive communication (chapter 9) with all the instructions to build your dialogue outlines and prompts for valuable conversations with generative AI.

RECAP

Gen AI can help you with a variety of self-management tasks:

- To speed up your personal productivity, you can use gen AI as a Co-Pilot to perform routine tasks such as managing email or summarizing documents.

- To improve the depth of your self-reflection and thinking, you can use gen AI as a Co-Thinker. It can help you review feedback you receive, analyze areas for improvement, and act on them for your growth.

- Some tasks might require switching between the two modes. You can start using gen AI as an efficient collaborator (Co-Pilot) and then as a thought partner (Co-Thinker) or vice versa.

CHAPTER 6

Gen AI for Personal Productivity

This chapter covers three Co-Pilot tasks using gen AI for managing yourself: **email management**, **time management**, and **summarization**.

By freeing up time from these labor-intensive tasks, you can concentrate efforts on more fulfilling work, improving your motivation, and productivity.

Email Management

While email is an essential communication tool, it can become a management quagmire. Long email threads can be time-consuming to navigate, requiring participants to sift through numerous replies, forwarded email, and quoted text to find specific information. This process wastes valuable time and hinders productivity. Additionally, these threads pose a risk of information overload, making it difficult to discern key points or prioritize actions and leading to decision fatigue and an increased likelihood of errors or oversight.

Gen AI models that are integrated with your email account (such as Google Gemini built into Gmail or Microsoft Copilot in Outlook) can help you manage your inbox more efficiently. They can execute tasks such as summarizing email threads and extracting essential information. Gen AI scans the thread, identifies key points, and generates a summary atop the email, including numbered citations linking to corresponding emails.

Moreover, gen AI can help you draft messages, whether a new email or a follow-up response, based on different tones and styles. Or you can improve the clarity and conciseness of a message. *You can ask gen AI:*

- "Shorten sentences and eliminate unnecessary information without losing the core message."

- "Simplify any technical jargon that may be confusing."

- "Clarify any areas that may be ambiguous or open to misinterpretation."

- "Rephrase to make the call to action more direct and impactful."

- "Detect potential unconscious biases to ensure the message is respectful."

- "Ensure flow is logical and transitions between points are smooth."

- "Fill in any gaps in the argument that might confuse the recipient."

GEN AI CO-PILOT IN ACTION
Transforming Email Writing

Many managers' emails are poorly organized and ineffective. This was the case for Franck, a young middle manager at a large technology company.

Franck received feedback that his emails tended to be unclear and filled with cryptic acronyms and technical jargon, making them confusing and difficult to understand.

Using gen AI as a Co-Pilot, Franck improved his email writing. He began asking gen AI to analyze his first drafts for readability; recommend simpler, less technical language while maintaining precision; and suggest revisions to improve conciseness. To clarify important messages for nontechnical audiences, he asked gen AI to take the perspective of specific readers, such as a colleague in the finance department.

Over time, gen AI became Franck's email coach, helping him to organize his thoughts logically in complex emails, craft compelling subject lines, and use a simpler, more effective style to explain technical concepts.

Time Management

As a manager, you likely have a heavy workload that requires effective task prioritization, yet you are beset by frequent interruptions and unexpected events. With a constant stream of communications, meetings, and responsibilities, managing your time efficiency is paramount.

Gen AI models that are integrated with your email account and team collaboration apps (such as Microsoft Copilot built into Teams or Google Gemini built into Google Meet) can help you manage your time effectively in many ways:

- **Get an overview of your week.** *You can ask gen AI* to show you a list of all your endeavors and scheduled time (for example, "What do I have coming up in the next three days? Give me a detailed list"). Gen AI can also organize your schedule into categories such as personal tasks, one-on-one meetings, work sessions, workshops, events, and time for yourself.

  - **Try this:** Ask gen AI to create a table with the breakdown of your meetings this week into the following categories [*specify*].

  - **Try this:** Ask gen AI to analyze your weekly to-do list [*share, link, or upload*], rank, and summarize the tasks based on the urgency and levels of importance you assigned.

  - **Try this:** Ask gen AI to scan your email for pending meeting invitations labeled "Urgent" and list them according to their deadlines.

- **Prioritize your tasks.** *You can ask gen AI* to make suggestions based on your to-do list and scheduled time (for example, "With regard to the finalization of the quarterly business review, suggest alignment calls to be scheduled with [*specify*] based on previous email exchanges [*specify*]"). Gen AI can also dynamically recommend changes to your schedule based on the priority of your tasks.

- **Gear up for an appointment.** *You can ask gen AI* to retrieve relevant information in preparation for a call, event, meeting, or workshop from recent email exchanges, chats, notes, or documents.

  - **Try this:** Ask gen AI to list your action items, as agreed in previous meetings or emails, and explain your expected role in the forthcoming meeting (based on an agenda you provide).

  - **Try this:** Ask gen AI to generate five talking points on the new product features that you will be discussing in a workshop with [*specify*]. Focus on a specific document [*specify*].

- **Participate on your behalf.** *You can ask gen AI* to summarize the content of a virtual session that you were not able to attend (for example, "If speakers shared a document, can you provide a brief overview of the content?"), including key discussion points and action items (for example, "Were there any next steps or deadlines assigned to me?"). Gen AI does so by attending the meeting for you, transcribing it, or analyzing the meeting recording (either audio or video).

– **Try this:** Ask gen AI to identify any specific questions or discussions you need to follow up on regarding [*topic*].

Summarization

Managers are inundated with an overwhelming flow of information from emails, presentations, long documents, and reports. Reading and distilling insights is a daily challenge.

Generative AI can help you efficiently summarize and interpret information. It is very versatile in dealing with different types of input and in creating output (for example, summaries can have different styles and formats such as tables, bulleted lists, executive summaries, short memos).

Suppose you need to review a 30-page document in half an hour. You barely have time to read the executive summary and first section. But you are worried that you won't catch the insights that might be relevant to make a sound recommendation. *You can ask gen AI to summarize the document and create a list of takeaways with references to the specific sections or pages from which it derived the information.*

- **Try this:** Ask gen AI to write a session abstract of this report for an upcoming event on [*specify*]. The abstract should highlight the report's findings and not exceed four paragraphs.

- **Try this:** Ask gen AI to compare two texts on the same topic and summarize all differences and commonalities between text A [*specify*] and text B [*specify*].

ADVANCED TECHNIQUE FOR SUMMARIZATION

For lengthy, complex documents, there are advanced techniques for prompting gen AI to create summaries. One of these is called "Chain of Density," which creates a series of summaries that contain increasingly detailed information.[a] This is achieved through repeated, iterative steps that incorporate additional critical details identified from the original document that were not included in the previous summary. As the summary becomes denser with information, it remains concise, keeping the same length.

Technique in Action

Juan is a middle manager who needs to summarize a long business report on company sales performance. Inspired by the Chain of Density technique, Juan built a chained prompt sequence to generate increasingly concise and dense summaries.

Prompt 1: Basic summary. Juan asks gen AI, "Please provide a concise summary of the key points from the sales report for the first quarter in no more than four sentences, focusing on overall performance."

Prompt 2: Dense, detailed summary. Juan asks gen AI, "Write a new, denser summary of identical length by including relevant information that was missing from the previously generated summary. Keep the same length. Avoid verbose language."

(Continued)

Juan repeats the second prompt a couple of times to generate a denser and enriched summary.

When applying this technique, remember to specify:

- **Summary length:** for instance, in the form of number of sentences

- **Depth of information required:** for instance, start from a broad overview and gradually request more specific details that were not included in the previous summaries

- **Accuracy:** for instance, ask gen AI to use information that is factually accurate (in other words, based on the report)

Be aware of text limitations: Depending on the gen AI model you are using, the length of the text you can insert in the input box (that is, the area where you type your questions or commands) may differ. If you have a long document to summarize, you can either provide it section by section to stay within the limit or upload it if that feature is available.

a. Griffin Adams et al., "From Sparse to Dense: GPT-4 Summarization with Chain of Density Prompting," Cornell University working paper, September 8, 2023, https://arxiv.org/abs/2309.04269.

Using gen AI as a Co-Pilot can streamline your personal productivity, but remember that AI-generated content can be inaccurate, misleading, or even completely fictional. It's your responsibility to scrutinize the output and maintain some level of manual oversight, especially for complex or sensitive communications.

Here is a list of questions to help you check AI-generated summaries and briefs. Although we recommend you to answer each question carefully, you could also engage gen AI itself in the debate:

- Is the tone of the summary appropriate for its intended audience and purpose?

- Are there any words or phrases that could be misunderstood or misinterpreted?

- Is the generated content sensitive to cultural and contextual nuances?

- Does the content inadvertently promote stereotypes or harmful narratives?

This chapter described how gen AI as a Co-Pilot can improve your personal productivity, assisting in tasks such as email and time management. In the next chapter, we will explore how it can also help you create content.

RECAP

As a personal productivity enabler, gen AI as a Co-Pilot can help you:

- Sort, draft, and organize emails.

- Manage your time more effectively.

- Summarize documents or presentations.

CHAPTER 7

Gen AI for Content Generation

This chapter covers two Co-Pilot tasks using gen AI for managing yourself: **text writing** and **slide creation**.

Gen AI can help you create textual and visual content to convey information or messages to your target audience, assisting you in drafting and editing. When you supervise the process and provide the right input and revisions, it offers faster and better-quality output.

Text Writing

You write on the job all the time: proposals to clients, memos to senior management, or reports to stakeholders. But how do you ensure that your writing not only gets your message across but also elicits the response you desire? Generative AI can help you improve the effectiveness of your business writing. Used as a Co-Pilot, it can analyze your text, proofread your writing for grammar and usage errors, and provide real-time suggestions for structure, clarity, tone, concision, and audience engagement. It can also organize your notes into a logical flow and write a first draft that you can iteratively revise and improve. It can help:

- **Create a structure.** *You can ask gen AI* to organize and logically structure your ideas into a clear narrative flow, suggesting pertinent subtopics or questions you may not have considered. Clarify the format to help gen AI know how to structure the outline for you, such as bulleted list or table.

FROM IDEAS TO A DETAILED STRUCTURE

To ensure gen AI produces the type of writing you are looking for:

Context. Describe the purpose, format, and audience for the text. Share your notes, and if not available, list your preliminary ideas with as much specificity as possible.

Organize. Ask gen AI to structure your ideas or notes in a bullet-point outline.

Articulate. Ask gen AI to elaborate on your ideas, flesh out each section (two or three sentences), and suggest other elements that may be worth considering.

Validate. Review the proposed outline and request modifications or corrections.

- **Write a draft.** *You can ask gen AI* to expand the outline into a full text or, if you are starting from scratch, to help you overcome the hurdle of "blank page syndrome." Give examples or specific phrases to help it generate more relevant text (for example, "Draft a new business proposal for client [*specify*] based on my notes. The proposal should mirror the structure and professional tone of a previous proposal I wrote for the same client [*share, link, or upload*]"). You can also leverage gen AI when you find yourself stuck; for example, "Help me rewrite this sentence and finish it by giving me three options."

  - **Try this:** Ask gen AI to give you specific examples for how you can improve your text [*share, link, or upload*] for a leadership review.

  - **Try this:** Replace these two sentences [*specify*] with a more concise and engaging introduction.

TO AVOID SOUNDING ROBOTIC, EMBRACE AUTHENTICITY

Generative AI should enhance your creative process, not replace it. You probably also want to avoid the uncomfortable situation of having a colleague, team member, or client ask, "That was written by gen AI, wasn't it?"

Declare your style. Describe your typical style by sharing what is uniquely you (for example, share text

(Continued)

67

excerpts that you wrote). This will ensure that the AI-generated content reflects your personal voice and tone.

Share personal insights. Add your personal touch. Use real-life examples, personal anecdotes, or insights that reflect your unique perspective. In certain situations, letting your text echo personal elements—such as humor—can strengthen the connection with your audience, making the communication more genuine.

Replace overly exaggerated gen AI language. Gen AI often constructs long, verbose sentences. To maintain authenticity and ensure the text remains true to your voice, remove words that don't resonate with you or that you wouldn't naturally use.

Seek feedback. For important documents, you may want to share your AI-generated draft with a colleague or team member. This will help you gather input on whether the text is authentic and has a genuine tone.

- **Strike the right tone.** *You can ask gen AI* to point out areas where the tone may be inconsistent with your intended message or the characteristics of the audience. Gen AI can make suggestions about the appropriate tone to use (formal, informal, persuasive, or informative) and adjust it accordingly.

  - **Try this:** Ask gen AI to check a particular paragraph for inconsistencies in tone.

- **Try this:** Ask gen AI to give you five variations of the paragraph to make it informal and
  friendly.

• **Customize content to your audience.** *You can ask
  gen AI* to tailor messages for specific audiences you
  are writing for. Gen AI can fine-tune the language,
  content, and examples by taking the perspectives
  of the different segments. Once the text is finalized, gen AI can also translate it into different
  languages.

  - **Try this:** Ask gen AI to write a message that
    aims at giving constructive feedback to a peer
    [*specify*], with the intention of enhancing your
    collaboration on future projects. The feedback
    should address the following key areas of im-
    provement [*specify*].

  - **Try this:** Ask gen AI to write an intriguing para-
    graph that conveys the benefits to employees of
    using a new company tool [*specify*].

  - **Try this:** Ask gen AI to simplify your text
    [*share, link, or upload*] for an audience that is
    new to the topic.

• **Streamline revision and editing.** *You can ask gen
  AI* to scan the text for grammatical errors and
  suggest more appropriate word choices to enhance
  textual consistency. Its capacity goes beyond mere
  typo detection. Generative AI helps you reconsider
  what you're saying and where you're saying it. For

example, "Identify parts where the narrative deviates from the central message, delete unnecessary details, and articulate unclear concepts more clearly."

- **Try this:** Ask gen AI to help you more concisely describe the text [*share, link, or upload*].

- **Try this:** Ask gen AI to suggest edits to your text [*share, link, or upload*] to make it sound more professional.

WRITE SMARTER, WITH OVERSIGHT

Generative AI presents opportunities for improving and accelerating writing, but it also carries risks. These include confabulations and hallucinations. To mitigate these risks, it is important to review AI-generated content. Gen AI may produce inaccurate, biased, or contextually unsuitable content. The output may, in other ways, not align with your personal and company values and objectives. Since gen AI does this in a convincing manner, you may fall into the trust trap. Remember to search for errors and intervene manually to correct them.

Slide Creation

Managers commonly make presentations to share information with their teams, senior management, clients, and stakeholders. Creating an effective slide deck can be even more challenging than writing an effective report.

When gen AI is embedded in your presentation app, it can support the creation of storyboarding content, generating slides, applying specific layouts and company templates, adding visuals, and creating speaking notes. Additionally, it can summarize a long document, audio, or video, and then convert it into a presentation.

You can ask gen AI:

- Transform this FAQ document into a concise 10-slide onboarding presentation.

- Generate slides on the new product launch, based on the notes taken during a client presentation.

- Refresh the content of this presentation with the latest data [*share, link, or upload*]. Maintain the length and structure of the original slides.

GEN AI CO-PILOT IN ACTION
Preparing a Slide Deck Under Pressure

Kate, the innovation director at a biotech startup, was gearing up to spend her afternoon preparing slides for a client call about the startup's latest gene therapy research. She had it all planned out, with the call scheduled for the next morning. But then the client rescheduled the meeting, leaving Kate with just one hour to put her presentation together. Faced with a daunting

(Continued)

task that would normally cause panic, Kate turned to gen AI for help. The company had just adopted an enterprise gen AI system built into the company's software suite.

Kate opened the slide creation app and asked in the chat to create a 10-slide presentation, based on her notes (that she copied and pasted into the chat), specifying the goal of the meeting, the audience, and the key messages. This step took her a few minutes. Gen AI quickly produced a first draft based on the company's template (that Kate specified). The output was a good starting point for Kate to tweak. She spent the remaining time to edit and fine-tune the gen AI-drafted slide deck, also adding her personal touch, and to rehearse for her meeting.

While gen AI can provide a good starting point and help create better slides faster, don't get the impression that creating slides can be as easy as pushing a button and being done in 60 seconds. Be aware of the risk of conformity—you want your presentation to stand out from others. Review all gen AI–created slides carefully and always bring a personal touch to your presentations.

HOW TO GET STARTED WITH SLIDE CREATION

Input. Ask gen AI to generate a presentation on a topic. Specify if you want it to create new content or use an existing document. You can also share a list of key messages to guide AI in the process.

Look and feel. Give instructions about the look and feel, such as the use of corporate templates.

Sequence. Make sure that gen AI storyboards one concept per slide. Edit manually and rearrange concepts if you are not satisfied with the suggested order.

Review. As with any AI-generated content, read over what it writes and edit if the content is inaccurate or inappropriate.

Add visuals. Ask gen AI to suggest visual concepts such as an informative diagram (like a mind map) or an interesting chart or image that helps make your point. Don't stop at the first versions that gen AI generates. Ask for several ideas for each concept you want to illustrate and select the ones that best associate with the messages.

Add multimedia elements. Ask gen AI to create interactive slides—for example, by mixing text, images, videos, and interactive elements—to better engage your audience. This feature will improve further as more gen AI systems become multimodal.

Add speaking notes. Ask gen AI to create talking points and suggest where you can add emotional texture, for example, opening with a story your audience can relate to or closing with a hard sell.

This chapter and the previous one explained how to use gen AI as a Co-Pilot to generate content and improve your personal productivity. In the next chapter, we will explore how to use it as a Co-Thinker to support your personal growth.

RECAP

For content generation, gen AI as a Co-Pilot can help:

- Improve your business writing, from proofreading an existing document to creating a new draft.

- Create slides from scratch or from an existing document, audio, or video.

CHAPTER 8

Gen AI for Personal Growth

This chapter covers two Co-Thinker tasks using gen AI for managing yourself: **self-reflection on leadership styles** and **soliciting feedback**.

Generative AI can assist you in establishing a regular practice, offering guidance in reflecting on your values, behaviors, and actions as a leader. To further support your personal growth, it can suggest approaches, tips, and techniques to gather valuable feedback and reflect on it.

Self-Reflection on Leadership Styles

Research suggests that the act of reflecting can make the difference between average performers and great ones. Reflection is about spending time thinking honestly about what you believe, how you act, and the results of those actions. It is a mindful and careful process that every manager should engage in regularly, yet most managers do not make reflection a habit.[1] Most are constantly on the move or are trapped in ingrained habits that are difficult to break.

When used as a Co-Thinker, gen AI can help you build a regular practice of self-reflection. By taking on the perspective of a neutral observer, it can contribute to a thoughtful conversation about your higher purpose, values, and behaviors. Gen AI can draw on popular and proven reflection theories and tool kits, guide you by asking a sequence of questions, share tips and examples, remind you that it's time to pause and reflect, and give you input on how to think about a particular habit.

CO-THINKING DIALOGUE
Self-Reflection on Leadership Styles

Co-Thinker's role. Gen AI acts as an expert coach, guiding the manager's reflection on seminal research such as the six leadership styles defined by Daniel Goleman.[a]

Setting. The setting for the dialogue is a one-on-one interaction in which the manager engages with gen AI as a Co-Thinker in a private environment, ideal for introspection and personalized guidance. Conversing with a machine can also mitigate the challenges of political dynamics, where fear can inhibit candid feedback.

Dialogue outline

[*Step 1*] Gen AI explains to the manager the six leadership styles and clarifies when to use them.

Gen AI runs a four-question quiz. The manager answers. Gen AI elaborates on the results of the quiz.

[*Step 2*] Gen AI asks the manager to select one style to focus the conversation on. Based on the manager's selected style, gen AI details the required emotional intelligence competencies that can help the manager nurture the chosen style. The manager provides feedback and selects one competence to be enhanced.

[*Step 3*] Gen AI asks the manager to provide a concrete example when the manager struggled to apply the desired competency. Gen AI asks for more details to better understand the situation.

[*Step 4*] Gen AI suggests concrete actions to start or keep doing in order to cultivate the chosen competency. The manager provides feedback on suggested actions.

Create the prompt. Visit hbr.org/book-resources to download an editable version of this dialogue outline. Make any changes you wish and then copy and paste it into a chatbot of your choosing.

a. Daniel Goleman, "Leadership That Gets Results," *Harvard Business Review*, March–April 2000, https://hbr.org/2000/03/leadership-that-gets-results.

While gen AI will probably never replace human coaches or mentors, it has the potential to work in synergy with them, complementing and reinforcing their efforts, especially when resources are limited.

THE NEAR FUTURE OF GEN AI
Coaching Chatbots

Gen AI is poised to transform the world of business coaching. Top coaches are already experimenting with AI-powered avatars, custom bots that mimic their knowledge and coaching style. One first mover in this space is Marshall Goldsmith's AI chatbot. The AI chatbot acts as a digital copy of the coach, capable of answering questions and providing advice just like its human counterpart.

These bots are built on LLMs and are customized with the injection of the coach's extensive literature, articles, and videos, effectively distilling their unique insights. To train the LLM, the coach is asked hundreds of questions, and the answers are meticulously edited so that the machine is able to accurately reflect the coach's unique style and insights.

The custom AI chatbot is designed to extend accessibility anytime, anywhere. For instance, between sessions, managers who are receiving coaching can engage with the AI avatar to clarify doubts, ask follow-up questions, and practice.

Proceed with caution because these bots, while advanced, may offer incorrect advice.

Soliciting Feedback

To be a good manager, you need to understand what you're doing well and where you're falling short. By requesting actionable feedback, you can learn and enhance your ability to make informed choices, adjusting your course as required.[2]

Your company probably seeks to foster an environment where people share constructive and actionable feedback. Even so, they are often reluctant to voice real concerns or criticism, especially to those in leadership positions. Your role as a manager is not only to confront people's reluctance but also to ease their discomfort in sharing their points of view. The art of asking for feedback and, equally important, the ability to receive it without becoming defensive are skills that you need to hone every day.

Using gen AI as a Co-Thinker can help improve your ability to effectively solicit, process, and act on feedback for personal and professional growth. *You can ask gen AI to take the role of a specialist in listening skills, self-awareness, and emotional intelligence, and engage in a conversation with you.* While this is a typical one-on-one setting in which you have a conversation with AI, the feedback collection process itself opens up to a group setting (one-to-many), where you seek input from team members, peers, and stakeholders.

CO-THINKING DIALOGUE
Soliciting Feedback

Co-Thinker's role. Gen AI acts as an expert coach, helping managers improve their ability to ask for candid feedback.

(Continued)

Setting. The setting for the dialogue is a one-on-one interaction, where the manager engages with gen AI as a Co-Thinker in a private environment, ideal for introspection and personalized guidance.

Dialogue outline

[*Step 1*] Gen AI asks the manager to describe the current approach to feedback collection from direct reports, including any difficulties or hesitations they often encounter.

[*Step 2*] Gen AI elaborates on the manager's answers and suggests methods for improvement based on good practices and examples. The manager comments and selects a method to further discuss.

[*Step 3*] Gen AI dives deeply into the chosen method and explains how to implement it, based on the context the manager provides, by giving concrete tips and actions.

[*Step 4*] The manager elaborates on recommendations for implementation and selects specific actions to start practicing the chosen method.

[*Step 5*] Gen AI shares pitfalls to watch out for and suggestions on how to manage the emotional reactions that may occur when the manager solicits negative feedback.

Create the prompt. Visit hbr.org/book-resources to download an editable version of this dialogue outline. Make any changes you wish and then copy and paste it into a chatbot of your choosing.

Gen AI as a Co-Thinker can not only support your personal growth but also help you become a better communicator. Let's explore that in the next chapter.

RECAP

For personal growth, gen AI can help you:

- Establish a regular practice of self-reflection, providing you with the awareness you need to grow faster and realize your potential.

- Understand how to seek feedback and respond effectively.

NOTES

1. James R. Bailey and Scheherazade Rehman, "Don't Underestimate the Power of Self-Reflection," hbr.org, March 4, 2022, https://hbr.org/2022/03/dont-underestimate-the-power-of-self-reflection.

2. Kim Scott, Liz Fosslien, and Mollie West Duffy, "How Leaders Can Get the Feedback They Need to Grow," hbr.org, March 10, 2023, https://hbr.org/2023/03/how-leaders-can-get-the-feedback-they-need-to-grow.

CHAPTER 9

Gen AI for Persuasive Communication

This chapter covers two Co-Thinker tasks using gen AI for managing yourself that require you to communicate persuasively: **speech preparation** and **job interview preparation**.

Gen AI can assist you in preparing speeches and talks that resonate with your audience, helping you become a better presenter by aiding not only in preparation but also in rehearsing and facilitating a post-speech retrospective for learning. It can also help you prepare for job interviews by rehearsing scenarios and anticipating questions your audience might ask.

Speech Preparation

As a manager, you frequently encounter the challenge of preparing and delivering persuasive speeches to diverse audiences, ranging from your own team to plenary sessions to external conferences and stakeholder meetings. It is easy to find many good practices for persuasive presentations in management literature and elsewhere (Nancy Duarte's *HBR Guide to Persuasive Presentations* is a helpful resource). However, the pressure of public speaking leads many to deviate from these principles and fall into common traps such as an overreliance on PowerPoint.

Using gen AI as a Co-Thinker can help you become a more effective communicator: preparing your speech for an important event, defining both the "what" of your speech (defining the storytelling, sharpening the messages and identifying potential weak points, preempting objections, leveraging metaphors and examples) as well as the "how" (setting the tone, the rhythm, eye contact, posture, gestures). The process involves a human-AI conversation to reflect on the audience's needs, frame the story, structure the narrative, and fine-tune the message, all while speaking with AI in your native language. In this dialogue, managers provide context and gen AI tailors suggestions to craft the right messages (storytelling, audience tailoring, metaphor selection, supporting point definition, balancing logical and emotional elements) as well as to improve the delivery onstage (mastering nonverbal communication aspects like voice modulation, pauses, and gestures).[1] The result is a presentation that not only effectively communicates your message but also profoundly connects with your audience, motivating them to reflect and act.

CO-THINKING DIALOGUE
Speech Preparation

Co-Thinker's role. Gen AI acts as a communication expert, applying the best practices for persuasive speeches.

Setting. The setting for the dialogue is one-on-one as the manager interacts with the machine in preparing the speech. However, at the end of the sequence, gen AI can suggest rehearsing the speech in front of colleagues and asking for their feedback. Based on the input from the rehearsal, the manager can return to the machine dialogue for further revisions. Additionally, the manager can record the rehearsal, upload the file, and ask the machine to provide feedback on the performance.

Dialogue outline

[*Step 1*] Gen AI asks the manager to provide contextual input about the topic and the audience. Based on this input, gen AI aids the manager in reflecting on the type of audience and suggests strategies to make the speech more relatable to them.

[*Step 2*] Gen AI assists the manager in framing the story—the beginning, middle, and end. The manager can provide feedback iteratively, adding or removing elements from the storyline as needed.

[*Step 3*] Once the story is framed, the manager provides additional information and details. Gen

(Continued)

AI suggests appropriate data, quotes, examples, analogies, or metaphors to reinforce the story's messages. The manager selects preferred options or asks for alternatives.

[*Step 4*] Gen AI develops appropriate wording based on the manager's input on tone and style. It suggests resonating keywords and appropriate sentences. If not convinced, the manager can ask the machine for alternative options.

[*Step 5*] After developing the speech content, gen AI provides recommendations to the manager on nonverbal components such as rhythm, eye contact, silences, gestures, posture, and voice. These recommendations also consider the target audience and the manager's style and preferences. For the elements where the manager may perceive difficulties, gen AI suggests tips and practices to overcome the barrier, referencing best practices.

[*Step 6*] Gen AI suggests three questions that the audience may ask during the speech. If these questions don't seem appropriate, the manager can ask for alternatives.

Create the prompt. Visit hbr.org/book-resources to download an editable version of this dialogue outline. Make any changes you wish and then copy and paste it into a chatbot of your choosing.

You can also use generative AI as a powerful tool for rehearsal or post-speech analysis and improvement. Before presentations, you can practice leveraging the voice-to-voice feature, if available. After, you can discuss your performance with gen AI and receive tailored advice by sharing a link or uploading the recorded rehearsals or speeches into the chat. AI can provide insight into the delivery, tone, and body language. This feedback loop allows for an evaluation of your presentation, enabling you to refine your skills by understanding what worked, what didn't, and how you can improve future presentations.

HOW GEN AI CAN HELP YOU BECOME A BETTER PRESENTER

To improve your presentation skills, consider leveraging gen AI as your coach for speeches. Here's what you can do:

Share your speech. Either upload or copy the link to the audio or video of your recent presentation or speak directly to AI using voice-to-voice features if available.

Ask gen AI to give you feedback. Gen AI can evaluate your speech and compare it to exemplary speeches. It provides recommendations on various aspects from the clarity of your message and engagement techniques to rhythm, voice modulation, and the effective use of pauses, as well as analysis of the gestures, posture, and stage movement.

(Continued)

87

Remember that generative AI can try to please you. When you feel that the feedback it gives you seems overly positive, ask:

- "Please provide honest and objective feedback."

- "Please identify areas of improvement. I'm looking for constructive criticism, not validation."

- "Please offer a fresh perspective that I may not have considered."

Practice the tips. Based on its analysis, gen AI can offer personalized homework and simulations to address areas for improvement and recommend readings to enhance specific skills, such as improving your effectiveness on stage.

Job Interview Preparation

A job interview is more than just an opportunity to land a new role; it's a chance to put self-improvement into action. Think of it as your own moment for gaining a deeper understanding of your strengths, weaknesses, and aspirations. Regardless of the outcome, getting an interview right—both in execution and in preparation—can help accelerate your professional growth. Gen AI as a Co-Thinker can act as a sparring partner and provide customized guidance tailored to your profile, interests, and values. It can help you take a deep dive into what makes you an outstanding manager and how to communicate effectively (internally or externally to potential employers).

In the interview preparation process, you can engage gen AI as your sparring partner to help you:

- **Extract insights.** *You can ask gen AI* to search multiple websites (such as Glassdoor.com), give you an overview of what to expect (company's culture, values, and work environment), and discuss with you whether you and the company are a good fit.

- **Prepare for the interview.** *You can ask gen AI* to assist in decoding the skills and qualities required in a job description, match your experience to those requirements, and help you craft stories and examples that highlight why you're a good fit for the role. It can also help draft or review your résumé and cover letter.

  - **Try this:** Ask gen AI to review your résumé [*share, link, or upload*] and cover letter [*share, link, or upload*], and discuss with you the key achievements and strengths to showcase during the interview.

  - **Try this:** Ask gen AI to compare the job description with your résumé [*share, link, or upload*]. Then have it help you reflect on any gaps, and preempt potential interviewer's objections.

- **Rehearse.** *You can ask gen AI* to simulate the interview, allowing you to practice high-pressure scenarios, tough questions, unexpected requests, or objections. Gen AI can also give you feedback on how to improve and provide recommendations for techniques to use. The voice-to-voice feature of gen AI models opens up opportunities for more realistic, humanlike simulations with AI speaking to you directly.

– **Try this:** Ask gen AI to help you prepare for a job interview for a role [*specify*] at company [*specify*] by providing three unexpected questions that the interviewer might ask about your leadership style.

CO-THINKING DIALOGUE
Job Interview Preparation

Co-Thinker's role. Gen AI acts as a career coach.

Setting. The setting for the dialogue is one-on-one as the manager interacts with the machine to prepare for a job interview.

Dialogue outline

[*Step 1*] Gen AI asks the manager to share information about the upcoming job interview, specifying the job title, the detailed job description, and company name.

[*Step 2*] Gen AI asks the manager to share their résumé and experience, and matches skills and qualifications with the job description, suggesting areas of strong fit as well as gaps. The manager provides feedback and comments.

[*Step 3*] Gen AI suggests adjustments to the résumé to best showcase the manager's qualifications. The manager provides feedback on suggested modifications.

[*Step 4*] Gen AI simulates a mock interview, starting from two common interview questions and increasing in complexity, including two unexpected or tough questions.

[*Step 5*] Gen AI provides feedback on the manager's performance during the interview simulation and suggests specific techniques to enhance communication skills.

Create the prompt. Visit hbr.org/book-resources to download an editable version of this dialogue outline. Make any changes you wish and then copy and paste it into a chatbot of your choosing.

This chapter and the previous one explained how to use gen AI as a Co-Thinker to support your personal growth and hone your communication and presentation skills. Let's now move to the next section about team management tasks that are enhanced by generative AI.

RECAP

For persuasive communication, gen AI can help you:

- Prepare your speeches by reflecting on your audience, thinking about the overall story and key messages, structuring the outline and co-creating a first draft that is in line with your style and personal touch.

- Hone your presentation skills by analyzing past speech performances, offering feedback on delivery, tone, and body language, and engaging in simulations and exercises for improvement.

- Prepare for job interviews by reflecting on your strengths, while anticipating objections on your gaps, and assisting you in rehearsal.

NOTE

1. For tips on choosing strong metaphors, see Carmine Gallo, "How Great Leaders Communicate," hbr.org, November 23, 2022, https://hbr.org/2022/11/how-great-leaders-communicate; for more on harnessing your voice, see Dan Bullock and Rául Sánchez, "Don't Underestimate the Power of Your Voice," hbr.org, April 13, 2022, https://hbr.org/2022/04/dont-underestimate-the-power-of-your-voice; for tips on looking and sounding confident, see Carmine Gallo, "How to Look and Sound Confident During a Presentation," hbr.org, October 23, 2019, https://hbr.org/2019/10/how-to-look-and-sound-confident-during-a-presentation.

Managing Teams with Generative AI

CHAPTER 10

Team-Management Tasks That Are Enhanced with Gen AI

Working in teams has become the norm. As more activities are conducted in collaborative environments, the nuances of team management—ranging from facilitating human interactions to fostering a sense of unity and purpose—are critical to team success. You play an important and challenging role in keeping your team productive and nurturing a psychologically safe environment that engages and encourages the creativity essential for high performance. Gen AI can help you manage and lead your team more efficiently and effectively.

TABLE 10-1

Team-management tasks enhanced with gen AI

	Co-Pilot	Co-Thinker
Managing teams	**Team operational support** • Meeting management • Goal setting and articulation • Task planning and reporting **Team creativity support** • Team composition • Idea generation	**Leading teams** • Crafting team purpose • Designing high-quality work • Facilitating conflict resolution **Complex problem-solving** • Problem framing • Root cause analysis • Problem storytelling

In team activities, a variety of basic yet time-consuming tasks such as meeting management, task planning, and reporting can significantly drain your energy as a manager if you do not manage them efficiently. Using gen AI as a Co-Pilot can help streamline these operational tasks, reducing their burden on the team and freeing up valuable time for higher-value and more creative tasks.

Managing a team effectively requires fostering an environment where creativity and inclusive team dynamics can thrive. This is not limited to R&D or innovation teams. It applies to any department and function, from operations to HR, that strives to innovate the way it works. Gen AI as a Co-Pilot can support you in nurturing team creativity by, for example, generating ideas for a brainstorming session or suggesting the right mix of skills on your innovation team.

Your role as a manager is also to develop a shared commitment, a purpose that keeps your team together and builds trust among people. Using generative AI as a Co-Thinker can help you reflect on how to create a psychologically safe and inclusive team environment in which you address and resolve interpersonal conflicts constructively.[1]

Finally, gen AI can help teams tackle business problems by guiding them through a systematic process. First, it helps formulate pertinent questions and consider multiple perspectives to frame the problem.[2] It can then help identify root causes across multiple dimensions, enabling a deeper understanding of the problem. Next, it helps organize potential solutions and assists users as they evaluate advantages and disadvantages. This process allows the team to converge on a solution that meets specific criteria. Throughout, the team engages in a structured dialogue with the machine, ensuring a reflective and iterative approach to problem-solving.

In the first two chapters of this section, you will learn how to use gen AI as a Co-Pilot for team operational support (chapter 11) and for team creativity support (chapter 12) with concrete examples of prompts that you can try. In the third and fourth chapters, you will learn how to have conversations with gen AI as a Co-Thinker for leading teams (chapter 13) and for complex problem-solving (chapter 14).

RECAP

Gen AI can enhance team-management tasks in both Co-Pilot mode (for operational tasks) and Co-Thinker mode (for structured reflections on team dynamics):

- Using gen AI as a Co-Pilot can relieve managers and teams of routine tasks (from meeting management to team composition) and support idea generation.

- Using gen AI as a Co-Thinker can serve as a source of reflection on how to effectively lead teams, helping you and your team think about a shared purpose, design high-quality work, and hone your problem-solving skills.

NOTES

1. Amy Gallo, "What Is Psychological Safety?," hbr.org, February 15, 2023, https://hbr.org/2023/02/what-is-psychological-safety.

2. Julia Binder and Michael D. Watkins, "To Solve a Tough Problem, Reframe It," *Harvard Business Review*, January–February 2024, https://hbr.org/2024/01/to-solve-a-tough-problem-reframe-it.

CHAPTER 11

Gen AI for Team Operational Support

This chapter covers three Co-Pilot tasks using gen AI for managing your team: **meeting management**, **goal setting and articulation**, and **task planning and reporting**.

Teams often spend a lot of time on administrative but necessary tasks such as planning, reporting, and meeting with people in other departments. What if you could free up a significant portion of your team's workday to focus on value-added activities? By using gen AI as a Co-Pilot, you can reduce the effort your team spends on routine tasks, increasing their motivation and productivity.

Meeting Management

Meetings are key to moving team-based work forward. They allow people to collaborate better and affect how individuals get their own work done. But meetings are often less effective than they should be. Poor agendas, lack of preparation, and insufficient postmeeting coordination can all derail the effectiveness of meetings. Generative AI, when integrated with your team collaboration apps (such as Microsoft Copilot built into Teams or Google Gemini into Google Meet), can help you improve the way you approach team meetings before, during, and after.

GEN AI CO-PILOT IN ACTION
Managing Recurring Team Meetings

Arun, a product manager at a tech company, was getting ready for the biweekly team sync meeting. Rather than spending an hour combing through updates from each team member, previous meeting notes, and relevant docs to put together an agenda, he leveraged gen AI as Co-Pilot.

To start, he asked gen AI to draft a 60-minute meeting agenda to discuss the latest product road map updates and new feature prioritization. He shared previous meeting notes and asked gen AI to scan the email thread with the team for further input.

Arun revised the drafted agenda by asking for small additions and reshuffling the order of agenda items.

Once the meeting started, Arun requested that gen AI takes notes.

At the end of the meeting, gen AI created a meeting summary with key takeaways and agreed-on action items. Arun reviewed and later shared it with all participants by email.

- **Before a meeting.** *You can ask gen AI* to help you plan and prepare for a meeting. Gen AI can create a time-boxed agenda (for example, "Draft a 60-minute meeting agenda based on my notes [*share, link, or upload*] or email thread with [*name*]"). It can also prepare pre-reading material (for example, "Summarize this document [*share, link, or upload*] into five paragraphs and suggest three questions that the reader should be able to answer after reading them").

  – **Try this:** Ask gen AI to suggest two to three good questions to ask a colleague expert [*specify name*] to prepare for a meeting on [*specify topic*].

  – **Try this:** Ask gen AI to create a 120-minute agenda for a workshop on [*specify topic*] in a table format with the following four headings: agenda point, title of agenda point, questions to answer, time for this agenda point.

  – **Try this:** Ask gen AI to include an additional item in the agenda [*share, link, or upload*] for discussing [*specify topic*] and conclude the agenda with [*specify item*].

YOUR ROLE IN THE MEETING, ASSISTED BY GEN AI

In meetings, many managers often fall back on familiar roles. Sticking to what they think is expected of them or what they've done before can perpetuate team dynamics and reduce the overall effectiveness of the meeting.[a] Starting from the agenda and topics of your next team meeting, gen AI can help you shape the role you want to play. Remember to share relevant information about your communication style and personal characteristics to help gen AI make better suggestions.

Try this:

Catalyst. Ask gen AI how you can stimulate team discussion and new thinking. Gen AI may suggest that you share a story or use analogies.

Challenger. Ask gen AI how you can challenge the logic, coherence, and validity of the main session's argument with data and evidence. It can help you create a list of questions you want answered, or it may bring to light the hypotheses you want to consider or reconsider.

Convener. Ask gen AI how you can communicate your belief in the team and encourage full participation in the discussion. It may provide advice on how to invite introverts to contribute more, providing you with sample language and even (if the gen AI model has voice-to-voice features) modeling an effective tone of voice to use.

a. David Lancefield, "Stop Wasting People's Time with Bad Meetings," hbr.org, March 14, 2022, https://hbr.org/2022/03/stop-wasting-peoples-time-with-bad-meetings.

- **During a meeting.** *You can ask gen AI* to take notes, transcribe the team discussion, track who says what, create summary notes to recap key discussion points, and produce meeting summaries in real time. This will free team members who would have been taking notes to engage more meaningfully. Or you can ask gen AI to improve team discussion and collaboration with lateral thinking ideas (for example, "Be creative and challenge us with three disruptive ideas"), different perspectives (for example, "Highlight potential areas of disagreement"), or supporting evidence (for example, "Search for data supporting the argument").

  - **Try this:** Ask gen AI to suggest techniques that can help you further increase the engagement of participants during the meeting [*specify format, participants, and topic*].

- **After a meeting.** *You can ask gen AI* to prepare the meeting summary, along with action items and due dates. For specific targets, gen AI can also create custom meeting summaries, such as a one-page memo for senior executives. Between meetings, you can ask gen AI to help follow up on tasks, track progress (for example, "Recap action items and due dates for each participant in the meeting"), and recommend topics and attendees for the next team meeting.

- **Try this:** Ask gen AI to list the areas where further discussion may be needed and any outstanding issues or questions that were unanswered from the meeting with [*specify name*].

GEN AI FOR INSIGHTS ON TEAM ENGAGEMENT AND DYNAMICS

During the meeting, you can ask gen AI specific questions on how actively engaged team members are in the discussion.

Try this:

- How balanced was the speaking time among participants so far?

- Who has not yet contributed by sharing their point of view on this topic?

- What questions can I ask to engage people who haven't talked yet?

- The conversation is stuck; what two questions can I ask to reactivate the discussion?

- Before we close, are there topics that have not received enough attention or feedback?

After the meeting, gen AI can provide a good basis for a team retrospective discussion on how to improve collaboration and communication, based on data collected during the meeting (who spoke, for how long, on what topics). It can also offer valuable insights for managers wanting to reflect on their leadership style and enhance their meeting management skills.

Try this:

- "Did I dominate the conversation by speaking more than two-thirds of the time?" or "Did I leave little room for questions or contributions from others?" Then, ask for techniques that you can learn or practice to improve your active listening skills.

- "Did I encourage team members to share concerns and raise issues during the meeting?" Then, ask for techniques that you can learn or practice to recognize and value diverse viewpoints and ensure that everyone has a chance to speak.

Goal Setting and Articulation

Helping your team set effective goals is a critical part of your job as a manager. Ambitious but achievable goals improve productivity, increase engagement, and help team members focus on the most important tasks.

Gen AI is familiar with a variety of goal-setting techniques, such as OKR, FAST, and SMART, and can help you and your team define, structure, and articulate goals effectively.[1]

- **Understand and select the right goal-setting technique.** *You can ask gen AI* to explain different techniques, provide examples, and offer clarifications. Once you select a technique, you can ask gen

AI to guide you through the application and share tips and common pitfalls to avoid.

- **Try this:** Ask gen AI to explain the objectives and key results (OKR) framework and share a sample. Try the same with the SMART or FAST goal frameworks.

- **Clarify the alignment with company's goals.** *You can ask gen AI* to assist in evaluating and rephrasing how team goals align with the company's overall objectives to make the relationship clearer and more compelling (for example, "Rephrase this goal [*specify*] to ensure that it directly supports the company's strategy [*specify*]").

  - **Try this:** Ask gen AI to analyze the link between our team objectives [*share, link, or upload*] and the company's overall strategy [*share, link, or upload*].

- **Detail goals and describe the tasks.** *You can ask gen AI* to articulate the team's goals (for example, "Based on my notes [*share, link, or upload*], detail the goals in two sentences and decompose each of them into three subgoals") and write task descriptions that avoid ambiguity by using clear, specific language and examples, making sure that each team member understands their responsibilities and contributions to the expected outcomes.

  - **Try this:** Ask gen AI to generate a summary of the project's goals [*share, link, or upload*] in a table with four columns: objective, tasks, individual or team responsible for implementing each task, and the deadlines associated with each objective.

- **Check whether the goals are well stated.** You can ask gen AI to evaluate whether a goal has been properly phrased in referring to your chosen goal-setting framework. Be aware in this scenario that generative AI cannot determine whether a goal is the right goal for your employees—only that it is structured correctly.

  - **Try this:** Ask gen AI whether a goal passes the SMART test following the SMART goal-setting framework.

- **Identify the right metrics to measure progress.** *You can ask gen AI* to provide a list of relevant metrics for each objective and highlight interdependencies among metrics for connected tasks.[2] If you already have a list of metrics, remember that you can ask gen AI to suggest overlooked metrics. In addition, gen AI can translate metrics into formulas and suggest how to measure them and how often to review them.

  - **Try this:** Ask gen AI to recommend four metrics to track the team's goals [*share, link, or upload*]: two qualitative and two quantitative ones.

Task Planning and Reporting

As a manager, you often formulate project plans to achieve ambitious goals while staying within an approved budget and on schedule. Most project planning and reporting tasks involve repetitive and sometimes tedious activities. When used as a Co-Pilot, generative AI can help you perform some of these tasks more efficiently.

- **Plan creation.** *You can ask gen AI* to organize and structure teamwork based on a project description and high-level plans. For example, "List project tasks and break them down into three subtasks. Suggest which task should be done first."

  - **Try this:** Ask gen AI to review each task on the project timeline [*share, link, or upload*] and confirm sequential logic ("Is each task listed in the logical order required for the project to progress?"), milestone alignment ("Are any tasks misplaced in relation to key project milestones?"), and task dependencies ("Are there any interdependencies or touchpoints between tasks? Please explain").

- **Plan visualization.** *You can ask gen AI* to create a visual representation of your project plan, including key milestones and the relationships between different tasks.

  - **Try this:** Ask gen AI to create a Gantt chart for a marketing campaign [*share, link, or upload*]. Remember to specify tasks such as market analysis (specify time, e.g., three weeks), campaign design (specify time), content creation (specify time), campaign launch, and performance analysis (specify time).

- **Project status reporting.** *You can ask gen AI* to draft reports for internal or external use based on the project's financial data, resources, effort required, and schedule. It can also enrich the reports with visuals. As with any AI-generated content, the report may not always accurately represent the project status. Therefore, it is imperative that you or a team member thoroughly review the report before it is finalized and distributed.

  - **Try this:** Ask gen AI to provide a summary of the updates and action items for a project [*specify*] based on the latest status report [*share, link, or upload*].

  - **Try this:** Ask gen AI to create a template to track project issues, including descriptions, status, assigned owner, and action items for resolution.

  - **Try this:** Ask gen AI to highlight any areas in the project status report [*share, link, or upload*] that lack rational or supporting evidence or that require further explanation and suggest improvements.

  - **Try this:** Ask gen AI to draft an email to a stakeholder [*specify*] to escalate a critical project issue [*specify*], outlining the impact and proposed solution.

Now that we have covered the operational support of teams, including tasks such as planning, reporting, and team meetings, we can explore how gen AI can support team creativity.

RECAP

For team operational support, using generative AI as a Co-Pilot can help you and your team:

- Improve the way you approach team meetings before, during, and after.

- Effectively define and articulate the team's goals, ensuring that members understand their responsibilities and expected outcomes.

- Create project plans and report on their status to a variety of audiences.

NOTES

1. SMART goals stands for specific, measurable, achievable, relevant, and time-bound. FAST goals stands for frequently discussed, ambitious, specific, and transparent. George T. Doran, "There's a SMART Way to Write Management's Goals and Objectives," *Journal of Management Review* 70 (1981): 35–36; Donald C. Sull, "With Goals, FAST Beats SMART," *Sloan Management Review*, 2018, https://sloanreview.mit.edu/article/with-goals-fast-beats-smart/.

2. Beth Stackpole, "Build Better KPIs with Artificial Intelligence," MIT Sloan School of Management, November 16, 2023, https://mitsloan.mit.edu/ideas-made-to-matter/build-better-kpis-artificial-intelligence.

CHAPTER 12

Gen AI for Team Creativity Support

This chapter covers two Co-Pilot tasks using gen AI for managing your team: **team composition** and **idea generation**.

Most companies would not be successful without the creativity of their people.[1] Creative teams are key to new products, better ways to do things, and happier customers. Every manager has an important role in making the most of these creative minds. Using generative AI as a Co-Pilot can help managers put together the right teams for innovation and provide the support they need to sustain the creative process during brainstorming sessions.

Team Composition

When you are running an innovation project, you must first make sure that your team includes the right mix of skills, backgrounds, perspectives, and personalities.

Second, you must create the conditions that allow people to interact productively in pursuit of the team's goal and contribute to their full potential.

Whether you are assembling a new project team from scratch or assessing the needs of a group you've inherited, gen AI as a Co-Pilot can support you in the many facets of the composition of creative teams.

- **Understand the composition of a creative team.** *You can ask gen AI* to help you identify the multidisciplinary roles required to establish a creative team, considering both the objectives and the different stages of the creative process, ranging from initial brainstorming to concept evaluation. This might entail a combination of roles such as strategists, designers, technical experts, and so on.

    - **Try this:** Ask gen AI to list the roles typically needed to compose a creative team working on [*specify*].

- **Articulate the skills needed.** *You can ask gen AI* to help you describe each role in terms of the specific capabilities and expertise that are necessary to the creative process. This can include a detailed breakdown of skills for each phase of the creative process.

    - **Try this:** Ask gen AI to create a job description for [*specify role*], including required skills and mandatory experiences.

- **Try this:** Ask gen AI to provide a detailed skill set in tabular format. The table should include the following columns [*specify, e.g., role, skills, profile*].

• **Check for the right mix.** *You can ask gen AI to ana-*lyze the team's composition to check for diversity in terms of skills, expertise, specialized knowledge, and previous experience. If it identifies a lack of diversity, you can ask it to highlight the missing elements and suggest other profiles that may bring those diverse perspectives to the team.

- **Try this:** Ask gen AI to list interdisciplinary skills that you may have overlooked in your draft [*share, link, or upload*] and that can enhance the team's capacity for creativity.

- **Try this:** Ask gen AI to identify any imbalances in the skill mix of your new project team [*share, link, or upload*].

- **Try this:** Ask gen AI if your team [*share, link, or upload*] lacks any important skills or diversity and to recommend how to address these gaps.

DON'T DELEGATE PEOPLE DECISIONS TO GEN AI

While gen AI can be effective at evaluating hard skills, previous experience, and qualifications, it lacks contextual and emotional understanding of

(Continued)

softer skills and people behaviors. It's your job as a manager to assess how well a candidate's work style (for example, team player, networker, communicator, influencer), soft skills (for example, emotional intelligence, active listening), motivation and personal goals, and life experience align with the specific needs of the project.

Idea Generation

Creativity is the ability to generate ideas, whether for marketing a product, rethinking an internal process, or solving a problem differently. Research has shown that the creative traits many assume to be genetically determined are in fact the product of one's environment: Creativity *can* be learned and nurtured.[2] As a manager, you play a key role in driving collaborative idea-generating sessions that draw on each team member's skills, experience, and expertise, and building a creative culture on your team. However, generating breakthrough ideas often entails an extensive brainstorming phase. You typically need to iterate through many options before you finally arrive at your most fruitful ideas.[3]

Using gen AI as a Co-Pilot can be transformative in its ability to augment the creative process by generating a wide array of ideas and providing fresh perspectives and insights to break through creative roadblocks.[4]

GEN AI CO-PILOT IN ACTION
Transforming Footwear Design

A design team at a footwear company used generative AI to quickly come up with and evaluate new product concepts. The team employed text-to-image technology to convert simple text prompts into distinctive shoe designs. These AI algorithms excelled at recognizing visual patterns and drawing analogies to create imaginative renditions of the team's text descriptions.

The team used gen AI to quickly and cost-effectively create numerous designs, showcasing a variety of styles, materials, colors, and shapes. This approach enabled the team to promptly identify the most favorable options to prototype and bring to market. Furthermore, the team could stay up-to-date with the latest trends and quickly adapt products to customer preferences by increasing the frequency of catalog updates in sync with style directions, rather than relying on prolonged traditional design processes.

This example demonstrates how generative AI can enhance the productivity and creativity of a design team during the concept ideation phase. The team provided detailed instructions and continuously assessed suggestions and output, while gen AI handled intensive visualization, enabling consideration of numerous creative concepts at the same time.

During a team brainstorming session, gen AI can enhance the creative process in multiple ways:

- **Breadth.** *You can ask gen AI* to generate a rich range of ideas, expanding the scope of idea brainstorming.

  - **Try this:** Ask gen AI to create a list of 20 potential applications for technology [*specify*] to address challenges [*specify*] in a country [*specify*], keeping in mind the constraints of the customer [*specify*].

- **Divergence.** *You can ask gen AI* to provide fresh perspectives by identifying patterns and relationships that may not be immediately apparent to you and your team members. This capability adds value to the brainstorming session by drawing connections between concepts.

  - **Try this:** Ask gen AI to analyze the common challenges your customers faced as reported in the last quarter's feedback [*share, link, or upload*] and suggest unconventional solutions by drawing parallels with different industries.

- **Clustering.** *You can ask gen AI* to categorize and combine ideas, leading to a more focused discussion.

  - **Try this:** Ask gen AI to review all the ideas generated from your last brainstorming session with [*specify names*] and categorize them into distinct themes such as technology, user experience, and sustainability.

- **Refinement.** *You can ask gen AI* to further articulate ideas, taking into consideration specific constraints (like budget, time, or technology) or requirements (like sustainability or accessibility), and create detailed descriptions of innovative concepts.

  - **Try this:** Ask gen AI to suggest ways to refine your ideas [*share, link, or upload*] to adapt to changing market conditions [*specify*].

- **Assessment.** *You can ask gen AI* to rate ideas on specific criteria such as novelty, feasibility, impact, and workability.

  - **Try this:** Ask gen AI to rate your team's ideas [*share, link, or upload*] based on innovation and feasibility. For each idea, generate a score from 1 to 10 (where 1 represents low innovation and 10 represents high innovation) and provide a brief rationale for the scores given.

- **Visualization.** *You can ask gen AI* to help you make concepts more tangible and concrete. By visualizing ideas with text-to-image capabilities, it's easier for team members to understand and build on each other's creative concepts. This is also important for inclusivity, allowing individuals who are more creative with visual expression than written or spoken expression to fully contribute their innovative ideas.

  - **Try this:** Ask gen AI to generate five images that represent a new product idea based on its high-level description [*share, link, or upload*].

- **Try this:** Ask gen AI to generate an image by specifying what you would like to see. For example, "Please generate an image illustrating the concept [*specify*] for the new product design within its context of use. Use red as the primary color for the concept."

THE NEAR FUTURE OF GEN AI
Beyond Multimodal Generative AI

Initially, gen AI models were largely unimodal, designed to excel at one type of data input and output (usually text-to-text). Then the advent of multimodality allowed gen AI to perform tasks that require any combination of different types of data, such as text, image, audio, and video. This is when gen AI models that respond to audio inputs (such as your voice) generate an image or video based on your request, seamlessly bridging the gap between different forms of content.

Looking ahead, there's growing interest in bringing these multimodal capabilities together in three-dimensional space. Managers may soon see the convergence of AI with other technology areas—virtual reality, augmented reality, and robotics. Imagine asking gen AI to visualize a concept in 3D during immersive brainstorming sessions, allowing participants to rotate, touch, and interact with the idea.

Although gen AI can be an invaluable ally as a Co-Pilot for creativity, humans must remain in the driver's seat throughout the entire process, making decisions on the most appropriate ideas for their specific business context. Remember to complement the process with other techniques, such as design thinking for ideation or customer exploration for concept validation, and find ways of connecting your brand differentiation and unique value proposition.

HOW TO RAISE THE BAR OF GEN AI CREATIVITY

Set clear objectives. Describe what you want to achieve, such as "I want to have a brainstorming session to rethink the go-to-market strategy of the product [*specify*]" and provide contextual information.

Infuse your brand. Explain what differentiates your brand from competitors and ask gen AI to consider it as a guideline throughout the creative process.

Establish content guardrails. Specify the boundaries within which you expect gen AI to create new ideas ("List ideas that are radically new and disruptive, not incremental").

Push lateral thinking. Tap into gen AI's ability for divergent thinking. If the creativity level doesn't meet your expectations, encourage gen AI further by saying, "Push the boundaries of creativity; I know you're capable of more."

(Continued)

Go beyond the first ideas. Don't just take the first few ideas that come up. Remember, gen AI doesn't get tired; ask it for more options.

Draw analogies. Take advantage of gen AI's ability to draw and analyze analogies from various sources to enhance a team's understanding. Ask for insights, such as "Show how other companies have effectively addressed a comparable challenge" or "Identify similar patterns in other industries over the past five years."

Define evaluation criteria. While gen AI can aid teams in clustering and evaluating ideas, the team must establish the criteria. For example, "Cluster potential solutions based on feasibility, novelty, and impact." Additionally, the team should provide explicit instructions and criteria on how gen AI should refine or merge ideas.

Remember that gen AI is a complement to team brainstorming and group ideation, not a replacement. It enhances creative sessions by increasing the speed, breadth, and variety of ideas, as well as assisting in organizing and encouraging divergent thinking. However, to use it most effectively, team members should be involved before and during the process. For example, suggest to team members that they spend 10 to 30 minutes individually generating ideas before they start asking gen AI. This will help ensure that they approach the team meeting unaffected by gen AI suggestions.[5] During the brainstorming process, they should exercise their critical thinking and contextual awareness in selecting and evaluating ideas. As a manager, your role is to make sure this happens. For example, suggest that team members assess the risk of conformity by spotting ideas that might be too common or similar to existing concepts.

Finally, remember to emphasize the importance of judgment in evaluating the feasibility, relevance, and potential impact of these ideas. Facilitate discussions that allow team members to reflect on AI-generated concepts, integrate their insights and experience, and guide the refinement of ideas into concepts. By combining the creative power of gen AI with the expertise of your team, they will be able to generate more innovative solutions.

RECAP

For team creativity support, using generative AI as a Co-Pilot can help you:

- Assemble creative teams by simplifying the process of translating project needs into specific skills and roles, ensuring a well-balanced team composition and helping identify the best skill mix to fill those roles.

- Foster idea generation by augmenting the creative process to generate a wide array of ideas and provide different perspectives to break through creative roadblocks.

NOTES

1. Richard Florida and Jim Goodnight, "Managing for Creativity," *Harvard Business Review*, July–August 2005, https://hbr.org/2005/07/managing-for-creativity.

2. Alessandro Di Fiore, "Creativity with a small c," hbr.org, March 19, 2012, https://hbr.org/2012/03/creativity-with-a-small-c.

3. Loran Nordgren and Brian Lucas, "Your Best Ideas Are Often Your Last Ideas," hbr.org, January 26, 2021, https://hbr.org/2021/01/your-best-ideas-are-often-your-last-ideas.

4. Tojin T. Eapen et al., "How Generative AI Can Augment Human Creativity," *Harvard Business Review*, July–August 2023, https://hbr.org/2023/07/how-generative-ai-can-augment-human-creativity.

5. "Don't Let Gen AI Limit Your Team's Creativity," *Harvard Business Review*, April–March 2024, https://hbr.org/2024/03/dont-let-gen-ai-limit-your-teams-creativity.

CHAPTER 13

Gen AI for Leading Teams

This chapter covers three Co-Thinker tasks using gen AI for managing your team: **crafting team purpose**, **designing high-quality work**, and **facilitating conflict resolution**.

As a manager, you need to lead teams by motivating them with a meaningful purpose and ensuring their work is of high quality. You also need to manage team conflicts, helping to resolve them in a productive and positive way. Generative AI can help you think and reflect on these issues by providing guidance, structured approaches, and methodological steps.

Crafting Team Purpose

Establishing a clear and compelling purpose is vital for bringing a group together as a true team. Linda Hill and Kent Linebeck say that a shared purpose acts as *"the glue that binds together a group of individuals. It is the foundation on which the collective 'we' of a real team is built."*[1] However, instilling purpose in a team is often a challenge for managers. Motivational speeches and mission statements can fall flat or even backfire if they are seen as insincere. True purpose comes from helping team members understand their impact on others and connect with why they love what they do.[2]

Using gen AI as a Co-Thinker can help you craft a compelling team purpose, giving clarity and motivation and driving people to action.

- **Guide a structured reflection.** *You can ask gen AI* to act as a methodological guide, facilitating a process to unveil the deeper meaning of a team and articulating a shared purpose statement.

CO-THINKING DIALOGUE
Crafting Team Purpose

Co-Thinker's role. Act as a leadership coach with experience in team dynamics.

Setting. The setting is one-to-many as the manager and the team members reflect about a clear shared purpose for their work as a team. During the dialogue, one individual (either the manager or a team member) types in the chat on behalf of the rest of the team.

Dialogue outline

   [*Step 1*] Gen AI asks the team to briefly describe the mandate, goals, and composition of the team.

[*Step 2*] Gen AI facilitates the team discussion on three key dimensions, one by one: *strategic aspiration* ("What do you want to achieve together and why?"), *creating value* ("How can you help those you serve achieve better outcomes and improve their lives?"), and *collective impact* ("How can you have impact beyond your direct clients or stakeholders?").

[*Step 3*] Gen AI interprets the team members' input and summarizes the team discussion. The manager and the team provide feedback about the summary.

[*Step 4*] Gen AI identifies common threads that form the basis of the team's shared purpose. The manager and the team validate the key points or request modifications.

[*Step 5*] Gen AI suggests a short sentence to distill the essence of the team's purpose into a few words.

Create the prompt. Visit hbr.org/book-resources to download an editable version of this dialogue outline. Make any changes you wish and then copy and paste it into a chatbot of your choosing.

- **Link team and company purpose.** *You can ask gen AI* to help you and your team reflect on the meaningful connections to the company's overarching purpose. For example, "Give three examples of how the company's purpose [*specify*] relate to the team's work [*specify*]." Conversely, you can ask gen AI to explain how the team's day-to-day activities contribute to the organization's purpose. For example, "Considering the team's achievement so far [*specify*], help us understand how it contributes to the company's goal [*specify*]."

- **Find the right team purpose.** A well-written and clear statement can help guide decisions and make team members feel more connected to their work. *You can ask gen AI* to offer multiple options for phrasing the statement to foster team's buy-in.

  - **Try this:** Ask gen AI to help you and your team evaluate the purpose [*share the statement*] against key criteria, such as authenticity, clarity, and inspiration.

Designing High-Quality Work

As a manager, you face the challenge of defining your team's roles, a task that is critical to producing quality work that is not only engaging and varied but also allows your people to grow. This involves giving each team member a clear role, providing constructive feedback, allowing for autonomy, cultivating a collaborative environment, and assigning a reasonable workload. Historically, this balance hasn't been easy. Decades of research have linked poor work design to stress, dissatisfaction, turnover, and low productivity. You can change this by creating meaningful and manageable work.

Using generative AI as a Co-Thinker can help design high-quality work that motivates your people.[3] *You can ask gen AI* to think together with you on key dimensions such as:

- **Autonomy.** "Help me think about warning signs such as reluctance to make a decision and constant approval-seeking."

- **Workload.** "Help me reflect on good practices that can optimize the workload distribution in my team." Or "List early and subtle signals of burnout I should monitor closely."

- **Mastery.** "Help me understand whether my team feels underchallenged and suggest techniques or good habits to stimulate them."

- **Collaboration.** "Help me reflect on how I can involve my team members in decision-making."

- **Engagement.** "Help me consider the signals of potential disengagement such as withdrawal from discussions and decreased participation in meetings. Suggest actions to overcome them."

CO-THINKING DIALOGUE
Designing High-Quality Work

Co-Thinker's role. Act as an expert in high-quality work design to increase people's motivation, well-being, and performance.

Setting. The setting is mainly one-to-one, as the manager reflects with the machine on how to design the teamwork better.

(Continued)

Dialogue outline

[*Step 1*] Gen AI asks the manager to explain the team's goal and scope of work, articulating the two main areas for improvement.

[*Step 2*] Gen AI suggests six factors to improve work design and asks the manager to select one. Gen AI then asks the manager to explain the reasons for the selection. Then, gen AI elaborates on the selected factor.

[*Step 3*] Gen AI recommends two work-design principles based on the selected factor. The manager may ask clarifying questions, and gen AI can provide more specific examples related to the design principles.

[*Step 4*] Gen AI describes three actionable steps to implement the two design principles and provides concrete examples. The manager reviews the actions, eliminating those that may not be feasible in the team's or organization's context.

[*Part 5*] Gen AI summarizes the discussion in a table that lists the factor, work-design principles, associated implementation actions, and two don'ts for each action. The manager provides final feedback and approves the table.

Create the prompt: Visit hbr.org/book-resources to download an editable version of this dialogue outline. Make any changes you wish and then copy and paste it into a chatbot of your choosing.

Facilitating Conflict Resolution

Conflict is an unavoidable and necessary part of collaboration. Teams with diverse perspectives and interests inevitably experience disagreements—and diverse perspectives are necessary for ongoing team performance. However, not all conflict is healthy; personality clashes and task-related disputes can become toxic if not managed properly. Unresolved conflict can wreak havoc on team morale, productivity, and relationships.

Conflict resolution is a critical skill for managers to address issues promptly and ensure that all team members feel heard and respected. Facilitating conflict resolution involves addressing issues promptly and impartially, actively listening to all perspectives, identifying root causes, separating people from problems, collaboratively exploring solutions, and following up to maintain a respectful and productive team environment.[4]

Using gen AI as a Co-Thinker can help you understand the sources of the conflict, explore resolution options, prepare for critical conversations, and productively resolve conflicts to rebuild team cohesion.

- **Understand the conflict.** *You can ask gen AI to* help you reflect on the root causes of the conflict by asking framing and contextual questions (such as why team members are arguing with each other, whether there are organizational causes, and whether it's a recurring pattern, a clash of opinions, or influenced by an external situation). Based on the contextual information and data you provide, gen AI can dive deeper to assist you in your investigation. Going beyond surface-level disagreements, you can ask gen AI to help you discern the fundamental drivers of the conflict, such as misaligned values, perceived unfairness, communication issues, or processing gaps, including those that you may have overlooked or not initially considered.

– **Try this:** Ask gen AI, "Suggest three questions to help me understand the origin of the conflict [*specify*]."

• **Suggest mediation approaches.** Based on the conflict situation and potential root causes you identified, *you can ask gen AI* to suggest the most appropriate mediation approach to effectively resolve the issue. For instance, if communication breakdowns are a key factor, gen AI may recommend facilitating face-to-face meetings in a neutral setting where all parties can air their differences. If misaligned values or different perspectives are fueling the conflict, gen AI may recommend an empathetic listening approach that focuses on understanding each colleague's goals, interests, and viewpoints without judgment. Additionally, gen AI can propose strategies to depersonalize the conflict, shifting the focus from the individuals involved to the underlying problem itself, while identifying areas of agreement and disagreement to find a solution that serves everyone's interests. By tailoring the mediation approach to the specific dynamics and root causes, gen AI can provide valuable guidance on how to navigate conflicts productively.

- **Try this:** Ask gen AI to compare two potential mediation approaches, illustrate the pros and cons, and suggest the one that best fits your situation [*specify*].

Facilitating Conflict Resolution

Co-Thinker's role. Act as a coach specialized in conflict resolution and mediation skills development.

Setting. The setting is one-to-one, as the manager reflects with the machine on how to best handle the conflict.

Dialogue outline

[*Step 1*] Gen AI asks the manager to describe the conflict situation, the actors involved, and the potential causes. Gen AI asks the manager to explain how the conflict has been handled so far and provides feedback.

[*Step 2*] Gen AI probes deeper, helping to reflect on potential pitfalls and suggesting complementary actions. The manager further elaborates on gen AI's recommendations.

[*Step 3*] Gen AI suggests three alternative mediation approaches. The manager selects one, and gen AI explains how to apply it, with concrete examples.

[*Step 4*] Gen AI simulates the selected approach, and the manager answers.

(Continued)

Create the prompt. Visit hbr.org/book-resources to download an editable version of this dialogue outline. Make any changes you wish and then copy and paste it into a chatbot of your choosing.

- **Provide narratives.** Based on the mediation approach you choose, *you can ask gen AI* to provide sample language—what to say and how to say it—to navigate conflicts effectively. This sample language can help you approach sensitive discussions with confidence, providing phrases and approaches that can help break down barriers, encourage open communication, and get to the heart of the conflict. You can ask gen AI to share examples that mirror your situation, as well as best practices.

  - **Try this:** Ask gen AI to provide sample language for initiating a facilitated conflict resolution session, including three phrases that encourage open dialogue and ensure a safe environment.

EXPLORING AND ESTABLISHING PSYCHOLOGICAL SAFETY WITH GEN AI

Psychological safety is a necessary prerequisite for productive conflict resolution. When team members feel safe to speak up, share ideas, and express concerns without fear of negative consequences, it allows for open communication, trust, collaboration, and risk-taking. As a result, you can address conflict constructively rather than avoiding or suppressing it.

To reinforce practices that promote psychological safety, *ask gen AI to*:

- Help you become familiar with the concept of active listening, empathy, and giving constructive feedback.

- Provide situational examples, concrete tips, and routines to develop psychological safety in daily interactions.

- Create a list of real-life situations that could undermine psychological safety, sharing common bad habits to avoid.

- **Debrief on mediation approaches.** *You can ask gen AI* to walk you through a retrospective. You can share your experience in applying the chosen mediation approach, discuss which aspects were easy to implement and which were challenging, and ask for tips or advice on refining your approach for future conflicts.

  - **Try this:** After explaining how you handled the conflict, ask gen AI, "Is there anything I could have done differently? Please explain."

We have covered how gen AI as a Co-Thinker can support you in leading your team. Now, let's move on to how gen AI can also help you and your team take a rigorous approach to discussing and solving complex problems.

RECAP

For leading teams, using generative AI as a Co-Thinker can help you:

- Find a link between your team and the company purpose, providing clarity and motivation and driving your team to action.

- Reflect on how to design high-quality work that increases the team's motivation, well-being, and performance.

- Understand the sources of team conflict, explore mediation approaches, and simulate how to productively resolve it to rebuild the cohesion of the team.

NOTES

1. Linda Hill and Kent Lineback, "The Fundamental Purpose of Your Team," hbr.org, July 12, 2011, https://hbr.org/2011/07/the -fundamental-purpose-of-you.

2. Dan Cable, "Helping Your Team Feel the Purpose in Their Work," hbr.org, October 22, 2019, https://hbr.org/2019/10/helping -your-team-feel-the-purpose-in-their-work.

3. Fangfang Zhang and Sharon K. Parker, "How ChatGPT Can and Can't Help Managers Design Better Job Roles," *MIT Sloan Management Review*, October 5, 2023, https://sloanreview.mit.edu/article/ how-chatgpt-can-and-cant-help-managers-design-better-job-roles/.

4. Jeanne M. Brett and Stephen B. Goldberg, "How to Handle a Disagreement on Your Team," hbr.org, July 10, 2017, https://hbr.org/ 2017/07/how-to-handle-a-disagreement-on-your-team.

CHAPTER 14

Gen AI for Complex Problem-Solving

This chapter covers three Co-Thinker tasks using gen AI for managing your team: **problem framing**, **root cause analysis**, and **problem storytelling**.

Every day, you and your team tackle problems. Unfortunately, the tendency to jump to conclusions without a clear understanding of the problem is all too common, hindering good decision-making and the ability to innovate.[1] As a manager, your job is to help your team spend the right amount of time and effort investigating problems before trying to solve them. Generative AI can be particularly helpful in the preliminary and often overlooked stages of decision-making. When used as a Co-Thinker, it can help you frame the problem to solve, discover root causes, and engage in effective storytelling.

Problem Framing

Problem framing, though often neglected, is critical for effective decision-making—to find the best solutions, you need to be able to ask the best questions. Framing a problem consists of determining the scope, context, and perspective of the problem to solve. It is challenging, requiring effort and proper guidance. Gen AI as a Co-Thinker can provide a sparring partner, helping your team in various aspects of understanding the problem and defining it. It can help to:

- **Support problem analysis and interpretation.** People have a common tendency to rely on experience and intuition when discussing problems and potential solutions. While this approach can work well for recurring, low-risk problems, it rarely helps when problems are high risk, complex, and novel. *You can ask gen AI* to assist in thinking about the problem in a structured way by searching for relevant sources and identifying roadblocks, correlations, and patterns that have occurred with similar problems in the past. This can help ground understanding of the problem in observable facts and data, leading to more-informed decisions.

- **Overcome confidence and confirmation bias.** *You can ask gen AI* to help you look beyond what you already know (or think you know). This reduces the risk of pursuing incorrect, inappropriate, or biased solutions in the future. For example, "Challenge our assumptions [*share, link, or upload*] and help us think about any potential blind spots."

- **Consider more perspectives.** Looking at a problem from different angles helps reveal unique aspects and insights, leading to a more complete understanding. *You can ask gen AI* to simulate the role of different stakeholders, providing alternative views on how they perceive the issue: interests, concerns, and impacts. For example, "Help us reflect on any critical stakeholders that we may have overlooked and explain your rationale for including them."

- **Diversify problem framing.** *You can ask gen AI* to provide a diverse range of problem frames, each offering a distinct perspective from which to approach the problem. This diversity opens the opportunity for alternatives. It sparks broad, critical team discussions, encouraging members to challenge and expand their thinking. By analyzing the alternative frames, you and your team can reflect more profoundly on the essence of the problem and determine which options to exclude from the analysis and the subsequent process for developing a solution.

HOW TO HAVE A CONVERSATION ABOUT YOUR PROBLEM WITH GEN AI

To start, describe the problem: background and scope, expected outcomes, key actors involved, and the most relevant barriers and constraints that hinder solutions.

Then, ask these questions to trigger a structured dialogue with AI and your team on a specific problem.

(Continued)

Ask gen AI to challenge you and your team:

- "What are we not seeing here?"

- "What else might be true?"

- "What evidence supports our assumptions? What else are we overlooking?"

- "How would our perspective change if our main assumption is wrong?"

Ask gen AI to suggest different points of view:

- "Wear the hat of other stakeholder groups: How do they see this problem?"

- "If we were our competitors, how would we view this problem?"

- "What would someone with beliefs opposite to ours say about this problem?"

Ask gen AI to reframe the problem statement:

- "Be creative in thinking about the problem and the related obstacles to address it. What are three alternative options to the problem frame?"

- "How would this issue be framed by a company operating in a different industry or sector?"

Root Cause Analysis

Once you have framed the problem, it's time to diagnose what is causing it. *You can ask gen AI* to act as a methodology expert and guide the reflection on your problem's root causes. You, your team, and gen AI can explore the problem thoroughly, peeling back the layers to uncover underlying factors and converging on potential solution approaches.

- **Understand methods and techniques.** *You can ask gen AI* to help you and your team understand various methods of root cause analysis such as the "five whys" technique, fishbone diagrams, fault tree analysis, and others. It can provide detailed explanations of each method, outlining their procedures, advantages, and applications. Additionally, gen AI can help you self-assess your knowledge by asking questions and sharing examples of real-world scenarios, helping you grasp the practical aspects of root cause analysis.

- **Apply a selected method for root cause analysis.** *You can ask gen AI* to walk you and your team through the various steps of one specific method so that you can apply it to your own problem. Once you describe the problem, gen AI triggers reflection following a step-by-step methodological approach. Remember, the ultimate problem solver is you and your team.

CO-THINKING DIALOGUE
Root Cause Analysis

Co-Thinker's role. Gen AI acts as an expert of problem analysis, applying the fishbone approach (also known as the Ishikawa diagram).[a]

Setting. The setting for this dialogue is a one-to-many interaction between gen AI and the team, including the manager. This is an example of a team meeting or workshop where gen AI acts as an expert and actively contributes to the team discussion. Depending on the gen AI model you use, it may also be possible to have a more immersive conversation using voice-to-voice feature.

Dialogue outline

[*Step 1*] Gen AI asks the manager to describe the problem the team is facing and to provide relevant background on the team and company. Gen AI elaborates and asks clarifying questions.

[*Step 2*] Gen AI asks the manager if they are familiar with the fishbone approach. If not, gen AI explains it, with concrete examples.

[*Step 3*] Gen AI asks the manager to list the categories that are relevant to the problem (for example, processes, skills, tech). Then it provides three overlooked categories. The manager decides which categories to include in the final list.

[*Step 4*] For each category, gen AI asks the manager to identify the root causes that may lead to the problem. Gen AI reflects on the manager's answer and integrates with overlooked causes.

[*Step 5*] Gen AI suggests potential investigation activities for each root cause. The manager provides feedback and integrates.

[*Step 6*] Gen AI summarizes the discussion in an investigation plan with five columns: root cause, action category, activity description, stakeholders to involve, and expected outputs.

Create the prompt. Visit hbr.org/book-resources to download an editable version of this dialogue outline. Make any changes you wish and then copy and paste it into a chatbot of your choosing.

a. Daniel Markovitz, "How to Avoid Rushing to Solutions When Problem-Solving," hbr.org, November 27, 2020, https://hbr.org/2020/11/how-to-avoid-rushing-to-solutions-when-problem-solving.

- **Generate diagrams and fault trees.** *You can ask gen AI* to leverage its multimodal capabilities, in models that allow it, to create diagrams or visuals supporting the textual analysis. For example, it could generate a fishbone diagram for the Ishikawa analysis or a tree diagram for fault tree analysis, or other schematic visualizations that may facilitate understanding and summarizing of the analysis of the problem causes.

> **THE NEAR FUTURE OF GEN AI**
> ## Multi-Agent Problem-Solving
>
> Research shows that increasing the number of AI agents can enhance gen AI's problem-solving capabilities.[a] Instead of relying on a single AI model, there are emerging frameworks (such as AutoGen by Microsoft) that leverage multiple agents to break down a complex task into manageable steps, leveraging various skills and autonomous problem-solving. As of this writing, multi-agent problem-solving requires coding skills that most managers don't have; however, given the rapid pace of advancement of gen AI tools, these techniques may soon be available to all.
>
> a. Junyou Li et al., "More Agents Is All You Need," Cornell University working paper, February 3, 2024, https://arxiv.org/abs/2402.05120.

Problem Storytelling

Storytelling is a powerful tool for problem framing and solving because narratives resonate with people's experiences and emotions in a way that technical frameworks cannot. By presenting problems through a story structure, it becomes easier to identify key elements, challenges, and potential solutions. The stories' inherent engaging qualities and memorability also help effectively communicate problems and inspire action across diverse audiences. Generative AI makes narrative-building skills available to everyone. AI can help you think in terms of stories, personalize your narrative for different audiences, and create multimodal stories that seamlessly combine text, visuals, and other media.

- **Craft the story as a "quest."** Storytelling simplifies complexity by framing the problem as a single overarching question, known as a "quest," which guides the path to the solution.[2] According to Arnaud Chevallier and coauthors, a successful quest comprises three key elements: a protagonist, an aspiration, and an obstacle. Gen AI models can help you think of the problem in terms of story ideas, plot lines, and narrative elements. It can also help you distill the main quest of the story. *You can ask gen AI* to help you reflect on the essence of the problem and suggest overlooked critical obstacles to solve it. The goal is to ensure that you are focused on the right "quest" to solve.

HOW TO FRAME A GOOD PROBLEM QUEST WITH GEN AI

Think of the problem as a quest. Ask gen AI to help you reflect on the problem [*specify*] in terms of a quest, using the following form, "How may [*person, team, or unit*] get [*solution's goal*], given [*constraints and obstacles to solve the problem*]?"

Do not give up on the first try. Approach the process as iterative. Follow up with more questions and share feedback. Ask gen AI to use simple and easily

(Continued)

understandable terms, exclude unnecessary details, and focus on one frame at a time.

Challenge and reframe. Ask gen AI, "Why would this not be the best quest to undertake?" or "Does this problem quest open up avenues for discussion or close down alternatives to one solution?" Suggestions may go from reconsidering some of the constraints to dividing them into separate quests, one for each specific constraint.

Stress test. Once developed, share the problem question with other stakeholders to gather new evidence, question the assumptions about causality, uncover blind spots, and identify new constraints. It also helps lay foundations for buy-in from key stakeholders: Once they agree on the framing, it is easier to involve them in developing the solution.

- **Personalize the story for different audiences.**
  Different functional teams may understand the same problem statement or question differently based on their respective expertise, jargon, and context. To ensure clear understanding and buy-in from all stakeholders during the problem-solving process, convey the problem narrative in language that resonates with the background and lexicon of each particular audience. *You can ask gen AI* to help you think how to better personalize the story about the problem [*specify*] considering the target audience [*specify*].

- **Visualize the story.** Thanks to its multimodal capabilities, gen AI can help you integrate multimedia, creating more engaging storytelling experiences. For example, a story may include descriptive text alongside visual elements like photographs, illustrations, or infographics to enhance comprehension and engagement in visualizing the problem. This occurs both in the framing stage (to understand the issue) and in the solution stage (to comprehend potential solutions and their implementation). For example, ask gen AI, "Help me think about how to incorporate a cartoon into the story [*share, link, or upload*] to engage the audience [*specify*] on the problem [*specify*]."

In this section, we have illustrated how gen AI can assist you in managing your team, serving as a Co-Pilot for tasks such as operational support, or as a Co-Thinker for tasks like team-based problem-solving. Now, let's proceed to the next section, which focuses on managing your business with gen AI.

RECAP

For complex problem-solving, using generative AI as a Co-Thinker can help you and your team:

- Reflect on the scope, context, and key perspectives of the problem to solve.

- Have a structured evaluation of the root causes, as well as the underlying factors.

- Think about the problem in terms of a compelling story for better communication and stakeholder engagement.

NOTES

1. Julia Binder and Michael D. Watkins, "To Solve a Tough Problem, Reframe It," *Harvard Business Review*, January–February 2024, https://hbr.org/2024/01/to-solve-a-tough-problem-reframe-it.

2. Arnaud Chevallier, Albrecht Enders, and Jean-Louis Barsoux, "Become a Better Problem Solver by Telling Better Stories," *MIT Sloan Management Review*, Spring 2023, https://sloanreview.mit.edu/article/become-a-better-problem-solver-by-telling-better-stories/.

Managing Business with Generative AI

CHAPTER 15

Business Management Tasks That Are Enhanced with Gen AI

As a manager, you steer a critical segment of the company, whether it is an entire unit, a product line, an operational function, or a moonshot project. In your role, you face multidimensional challenges that require a blend of operational expertise and strategic vision. On the one hand, you need to analyze data to make informed decisions and improve the odds of success. On the other, you're responsible for evaluating growth options, developing a compelling business case, and navigating strategic initiatives that will shape the company's long-term trajectory. Gen AI can help you augment capabilities on both operational and strategic fronts.

TABLE 15-1

Business management tasks enhanced with gen AI

	Co-Pilot	Co-Thinker
Managing business	**Data analysis support** • Information search • Data analysis and visualization **Customer insights** • Research design and analysis • Synthetic research	**Business case development** • Stakeholder perspectives • Evaluating trade-offs • Risk identification and mitigation **Strategic decisions** • Formulating business strategy • Evaluating innovative concepts • Assessing supply chain strategy

Using gen AI as a Co-Pilot can speed up time-consuming and data-intensive analysis. Just as you use generative AI to edit and enhance text-based documents, you can apply these capabilities to analyze data. Gen AI can quickly process large data sets and extract valuable insights to inform your decision-making. Data analysis and customer insights are typically preparatory work for informing subsequent tasks to be executed with gen AI as a Co-Thinker, such as developing business cases or formulating strategies.

These are sophisticated tasks that require thinking and reflection. Throughout these processes, leveraging gen AI as a Co-Thinker can help you ponder various dimensions and outcomes. You can prompt gen AI to guide you through methodological questions, suggest different stakeholder perspectives, and evaluate trade-offs. If you are a financial manager, gen AI can take the perspective of an investor and help you identify the elements of your company's performance that an investor would focus on.

If you are a product manager, gen AI can become your thought partner in evaluating an innovative concept. If you are a supply chain manager, gen AI can help you think about emerging trends and their potential impact on your operations strategy.

In the first part of this section, you will learn how to use gen AI as a Co-Pilot for data analysis support (chapter 16) and for customer insights (chapter 17) with concrete examples of prompts that you can try. In the second part of this section, you will learn how to use gen AI as a Co-Thinker for a business case (chapter 18) and strategic decisions (chapter 19) with instructions to build your dialogue outline for a value-added conversation with gen AI and to transform your outline into immediately executable prompts.

RECAP

Gen AI can enhance business management in both Co-Pilot mode (for data analysis and research-related tasks) and Co-Thinker mode (for thinking through more strategic options and business decisions).

- Using gen AI as a Co-Pilot can support data-intensive activities and customer research in ways ranging from survey design to synthetic data generation.

- Using gen AI as a Co-Thinker can help you ponder complex business situations. For example, when formulating a strategy for a business unit or evaluating the impact of technology trends on operations.

CHAPTER 16

Gen AI for Data Analysis Support

This chapter covers two Co-Pilot tasks using gen AI for managing your business: **information search** and **data analysis and visualization**.

Scrolling through web pages of search results or struggling with complicated formulas in spreadsheets can be frustrating and even hinder your productivity. Imagine simply talking to your search engine, asking for elaboration on the information you need, or telling your spreadsheet what data to crunch. With generative AI, managers can quickly find answers, extract findings, and understand data, turning previously time-consuming tasks into simple human-AI interactions. Think of gen AI as a data science–savvy collaborator to support you through the entire process, from analysis to insight.

Information Search

All managers need access to information to make good decisions. Do you remember the old days of searching through books in libraries? The internet revolution, with search engines and keywords, made research much easier and faster. Now, generative AI is changing the paradigm again. Managers can ask gen AI questions and receive elaborate information presented in natural language in a way that is both intuitive and efficient, with the possibility of asking follow-up questions and diving deeper into topics. And it's not just for web searches. Thanks to gen-AI-powered chat interfaces, managers can now engage in a more interactive and personalized experience when they search information within their company's knowledge base. Instead of just listing links to internal documents or folders, gen AI provides results in the form of direct answers or summaries to questions.

Generative AI as a Co-Pilot can transform traditional information retrieval from various sources:

- **Web knowledge.** When it's integrated with traditional browsers, *you can ask gen AI* to scan the web, extract key findings, and cite sources directly in the response. You can formulate complex questions, rather than using mere keywords, to narrow the search to specific sources, such as news articles, industry reports, or YouTube videos. Instead of visiting multiple websites, gen AI does it for you quickly and creates a summary of findings, greatly speeding up your web search.

- **Try this:** Ask gen AI to summarize the latest developments in technology [*specify*] for supply chain management over the past 12 months. Focus on benefits, challenges, and real-world applications, citing key studies and articles from reputable sources [*specify*].

ALWAYS CHECK THE RELIABILITY OF CITED SOURCES

A notable pitfall of gen AI systems, which was especially pronounced in their early days, is the tendency to fabricate citations, sources, or even entire studies and papers.

To counteract this issue, some specialized gen AI systems incorporate guardrails of "humility": These are designed to recognize and admit their limitations, explicitly stating when information is not available or when the AI cannot provide a definitive answer. This approach helps to mitigate the risk of misinformation by ensuring the reliability and origin of the information they receive. However, the final check and verification remains the responsibility of the human.

Another useful tactic is to incorporate instructions such as "Please do not fabricate sources" into your prompt (although this instruction will not completely eliminate the risk).

- **Company knowledge.** When it's connected to your company's internal knowledge base, *you can ask gen AI* to quickly search through internal databases, documents, and reports. In addition to providing a list of sources or links, it can summarize key points and uncover connections and findings across available sources. Managers can type in questions such as "What solutions to problem [*specify*] were tried in the past?" and gen AI surfaces relevant information based on available documents and condenses findings into a bullet-point list or short paragraph.

  - **Try this:** Ask gen AI for a list of projects undertaken in the last three years related to the adoption of technology [*specify*] for application [*specify*] and summarize the commonalities and differences in the implementation approach.

  - **Try this:** Ask gen AI to find all files shared with [*specify name*] in the past month on topic [*specify*].

  - **Try this:** Ask gen AI to find all files that your colleague [*specify*] has commented on.

- **Expert knowledge.** *You can ask gen AI* to turn the vast amount of information shared in chats and virtual team discussions into organized and easy-to-use resources. This is particularly helpful when you oversee or participate in communities or groups of experts where a great deal of valuable knowledge is shared. You can request that gen AI cluster and summarize information shared by sub-topic, identify trending and widely discussed questions, and provide the names of active contributors you may want to contact or follow up with.

HOW GEN AI CAN HELP COMMUNITY MANAGERS

In every organization, there are communities of experts: groups of people sharing knowledge and passion for a topic. If you are a community manager, generative AI models that are built into the software products you use every day (such as Microsoft 365 Copilot for Office and Google Gemini for Workspace) can help you in multiple ways:

Conversations extraction. Ask gen AI to monitor the community chats and extract top insights and learnings, which you can later share in weekly digests or newsletters.

Theme detection. Request that gen AI identify recurring themes, trends, and questions. This involves breaking down conversations to understand the context and categorizing the information efficiently.

Knowledge organization. Instruct gen AI to synthesize the identified themes into a structured format. Whether it's creating knowledge base articles, summary reports, or repository entries, the AI will include critical insights and expert opinions for quick reference.

(Continued)

Enhance accessibility. Request that gen AI integrate the summarized knowledge into your company's internal knowledge base, making it easily searchable through keywords or thematic queries.

Expert mapping. Ask gen AI to recognize and tag members who contribute valuable insights on specific topics, creating an internal map of expertise. This links particular themes or queries directly to the experts in your community.

Data Analysis and Visualization

As a manager, you need to make data-driven decisions without getting bogged down by the technical complications of data cleaning, analysis, and visualization. In the same way you use generative AI to edit and improve text-based documents, you can also apply these AI capabilities to data analysis. Imagine talking with your spreadsheet in real time and instructing gen AI to perform tasks for you.

GEN AI CO-PILOT IN ACTION
Streamlining Data Analysis

Lina, a marketing manager for a consumer products company, is preparing her quarterly business review presentation. She has a lot of data to clean and analyze from multiple spreadsheets. In the past, she and her team would have spent many hours consolidating, preparing, and analyzing the data. Thanks to gen AI's integration with the spreadsheet software, they now have valuable additional support.

Gen AI can combine data sets, check for missing or inconsistent values, and prepare a clean, consolidated version for structured analysis. Lina and her team can now interact with the consolidated data set, asking gen AI to identify key trends and formulate key messages to include in the business review presentation.

Lina and her team can also ask gen AI to help visualize the quarterly numbers. Gen AI recommends two types of charts, and Lina selects the preferred one for gen AI to create.

- **Read and clean data.** *You can ask gen AI* to read the data, describe its contents, perform preliminary checks (such as identifying missing or null values and potentially incorrect calculations or formulas), and prepare the data set (in the form of a spreadsheet) for analysis. Not only does this free up time and simplify data cleaning, but it also enhances the integrity and reliability of the analyses performed on the data.

  - **Try this:** Ask gen AI to describe the contents of the data set [*share, link, or upload*]. Then ask gen AI to clean the data set by removing duplicates, normalizing values across various measurement scales, and correcting inconsistencies in variable categorization.

DOUBLE-CHECK THE OUTPUT
GENERATED BY GEN AI

Despite the sophistication of gen AI's data analysis, vigilance is key. Errors do occur, so it is imperative that you remind your team to regularly verify the accuracy of the output.

Verification can happen at different levels, depending on the complexity of the analysis and on the associated risk and necessary control:

- **Machine check.** Ask AI to reevaluate the output and highlight potential anomalies or inconsistencies. Although gen AI may not always recognize or self-correct, this practice helps you develop a habit of challenging AI work.

- **Individual check.** Ask yourself if gen AI's results seem logically coherent or if there are unexpected outliers or data inconsistency.

- **Team check.** Schedule a time for the team to review and critically assess the output together, ensuring a range of expertise and perspectives are considered.

- **Retrospective analysis.** After task or project completion, conduct small sessions to reflect on the error patterns and how to spot them quickly next time. Also, keep track of the most effective prompts and instructions that consistently lead to good quality output.

- **Work with data and extracting insights.** *You can ask gen AI* to perform structured analyses of databases or spreadsheets that you share, link, or upload. Whether identifying trends, segmenting markets, evaluating performance, or calculating metrics, gen AI can turn your text or voice-based requests into results.

  - **Try this:** Ask gen AI to calculate the total sales for product [*specify*].

  - **Try this:** Ask gen AI to calculate the total advertising expenditure for [*specify country/region*] in the last quarter.

  - **Try this:** Ask gen AI to split customer data into three demographics [*specify*].

HOW TO TALK TO YOUR SPREADSHEET IN PRACTICE

Gen AI can answer various types of requests once you upload the data set you want to analyze; for example:

- **Ranking.** "Highlight the top five values in the revenues column and the highest values in the products-sold column to identify the best performers."

- **Sorting.** "Cluster items from largest to smallest to identify areas to focus on."

- **Filtering.** "Filter the sales data to display only transactions that occurred in the region [*specify*]."

(Continued)

- **Calculations.** "Add a column that calculates the total profit for each marketing campaign to evaluate our return on investment."

- **Trend recognition.** "Analyze the data set, which contains [*specify*], to identify key trends. Define key trends as [*specify criteria, e.g., patterns over time or correlations between variables*]."

- **Pivots.** "Create a pivot table to plot sales by category over time and show total sales for each service, identifying market trends and service performance."

- **Pattern recognition.** "Look for patterns in purchasing behaviors over last two quarters to inform our marketing strategy."

- **Sensitivity analysis.** "Perform a sensitivity analysis on price changes to understand the impact on sales volume and profit margins."

- **Translate data into visuals.** *You can ask gen AI* to visualize data in a specific format (for example, "Generate a bar chart showing product revenue for the last quarter, grouped by region"). But generative AI does more than just speed up chart creation. You can ask for suggestions on the best ways to visualize your data, including the most effective chart types and design features such as color palettes, fonts, and sizes that will make your visualizations more insightful and compelling (for example, "What color scheme and design choices would best enhance the readability of this visual?").

- **Try this:** Ask gen AI to suggest three appropriate data visualization types for conveying this message [*specify*]. Then, request a recommendation on the most suitable option, along with a rationale for its selection.

- **Try this:** Ask gen AI, "Which data points should be highlighted in this visual to draw attention to the most important insights [*specify*]?"

- **Try this:** Ask gen AI to tailor the visualization for a specific audience [*specify, for example, technical experts, executives, wider organization*].

- **Communicate your data.** *You can ask gen AI* to craft textual descriptions, captions, or simple explanations for the visuals it created. By adding narratives to your charts and graphs, gen AI helps you turn plain data into something much more compelling. This makes the data storytelling more informative and engaging.

  - **Try this:** Ask gen AI, "What's the key message I can tell on this chart? Create two sentences."

  - **Try this:** Ask gen AI, "What questions can I pose to the audience to engage them further with the data, encouraging them to explore its implications?"

- **Try this:** Ask gen AI to frame the insights from this chart in a way that connects with the audience [*specify*].

While gen AI as a Co-Pilot can enhance data analysis and visualization productivity, it is not a silver bullet. You can get suggestions for formula columns within seconds, but they may not always be relevant or applicable to your context. For example, gen AI might calculate customer satisfaction in a way that does not reflect the standard measures of your industry. Gen AI can offer valuable support, but achieving meaningful results always demands your critical thinking, domain expertise, and contextualization.

We have covered how gen AI as a Co-Pilot can support your data analysis; now let's move on to how it can assist in generating customer insights by drawing on traditional customer research or a more advanced technique that gen AI makes possible—synthetic research.

RECAP

For data analysis, using gen AI as a Co-Pilot can help you:

- Retrieve information from the internet or from internal knowledge databases using simple, plain-language conversations with the machine.

- Analyze your spreadsheet, extract trends and patterns, and present them in appropriate and effective visualizations.

CHAPTER 17

Gen AI for Customer Insights

This chapter covers two Co-Pilot tasks using gen AI for managing your business: **research design and analysis** and **synthetic research**.

Successful managers deeply understand their customers' needs and fulfill them better than anyone else. They gather insights by speaking with customers directly or through surveys; they observe and interact with them while they use products. Generative AI can help any manager design and prepare customer research, interpret data, and extract key findings. It can also generate synthetic user data for early-stage assumption testing when traditional methods fell short or customer research is difficult to collect.

Research Design and Analysis

Generative AI as a Co-Pilot can improve the efficiency of data collection and analysis in different ways.

- **Survey creation.** *You can ask gen AI* to define the interview structure and survey questions, and to suggest how to optimize your sampling method. Based on your goals and specific audiences, gen AI can also personalize some questions.

  - **Try this:** Ask gen AI to draft a 10-question multiple choice survey that effectively measures key areas of interest in your research [*specify*], such as customer experience, product quality, and repurchase intention.

THE NEAR FUTURE OF GEN AI
Dynamic Chat-Based Surveys

No longer distributed via email or hosted on a website, this novel approach will enable respondents to interact with an AI chatbot that adapts the questions based on previous answers, resulting in a personalized survey experience for each respondent. Imagine the richness of a focus group with the efficiency of an automated survey. This can take the collection of real-time customer feedback on digital products to the next level. It will help managers better understand customer engagement, drop-off rates, or issues with the product's digital experience.

- **Analyze qualitative research data.** *You can ask gen AI* to categorize, analyze, and interpret both structured and unstructured data that you share, link, or upload (in the form of free text responses), such as customer interview transcripts, product reviews, and social media comments. AI can identify patterns, highlight preferences or recurring concerns, and even assess sentiment and emotional tone.

  - **Try this:** If you or your team have conducted a series of customer interviews, ask gen AI to summarize each interview with two key points and identify common themes and differences among interviewees.

  - **Try this:** Ask gen AI to analyze the database with all the product reviews [*share, link, or upload*] received in the last period of time [*specify*], categorize them, and summarize main patterns, based on recurring keywords.

Whenever you are considering your customer research plan, remember that your use of gen AI with company and/or customer data must always comply with your organization's policies.

HOW GEN AI CAN ANALYZE YOUR CUSTOMER FEEDBACK

Gen AI can support managers in the analysis of subjective information found in the text it processes.

Try this: Share a document (for example, social media posts related to a new product, collected in the last 10 days), and ask gen AI to:

- Clean the data for analysis, such as removing hashtags, mentions, and nonalphabetic characters, and correcting typos.

- Categorize each tweet's sentiment as positive, negative, or neutral. Also, provide the percentage distribution of each sentiment category.

- List the 10 most frequently occurring words and phrases in the positive, negative, and neutral tweets separately.

- Explain how the identified words and phrases contribute to the sentiment in each category.

- Provide a summary, including any relevant customer suggestions.

However, when text is highly specialized and nuanced, such as technical product reviews or detailed service complaints, dedicated advanced tools for sentiment detection will deliver better results.

THE HUMAN ELEMENT IN CUSTOMER INSIGHTS

Insight generation is predominantly a human skill. Do not rely solely on technology to interpret complex nuances, understand contextual subtleties, or make judgment calls that require deep domain expertise and emotional intelligence.

Synthetic Research

Good-quality data is essential to innovating and delivering more customer-centric products or services. However, there are real-world data access challenges that can hinder this: from privacy and regulatory compliance to bias and limited availability.

What can managers do if they can't efficiently reach their customers or certain segments to collect the data they need?

Generative AI can help. It can create artificial customer data (in the form of text-based, tabular, or image-based data) that mimics the characteristics and behavior of real data, acting as a useful proxy for real customers.

DIFFERENT TYPES OF SYNTHETIC DATA

Fully synthetic. Data generated by AI algorithms based on predefined parameters, without the use of real data (as an input). This applies to situations where data is difficult to find or not available. For example, imagine your team is researching a new drug to treat a specific rare

(Continued)

disease. If there isn't enough real-world data on how the drug interacts with the human body, gen AI can create a synthetic data set to run simulations.

Partially synthetic. Data generated by AI algorithms mixing real and synthetic data. This is useful when real data is not sufficient (quantity) or has some limitations (noise, errors, gaps), for example, artificially generated images generated from real-life pictures or targeted recommendations created for customers with limited purchase history.

Product development and testing is one area where synthetic data is increasingly being used. Based on patterns and relationships learned from actual data, gen AI can create synthetic customer groups that can be used to test, for example, how certain types of customers would react to a new product feature.

You can ask gen AI to simulate customer responses to changes in service pricing, providing insights into potential market reactions, or to test which customers, with which characteristics, will be attracted to the new product. This can enhance the initial phases of exploration, piloting, and testing of research ideas.

- **Try this:** Ask gen AI to act as a proxy for your customer [*specify*] in geography [*specify*], based on your predefined personas [*share, link, or upload*], and simulate reactions to a change in product feature [*specify*], under a range of conditions [*detail*].

- **Try this:** Ask gen AI to test content variations on a synthetic customer audience [*specify*] to determine what resonates before launching the advertising campaign [*share, link, or upload*].

- **Try this:** Ask gen AI to simulate the reactions of two customer groups [*specify*] using your e-commerce platform to a proposed user interface overhaul that includes a new checkout process [*specify*].

- **Try this:** Ask gen AI to simulate the most likely intangible variables to forming a long-term relationship between the customer [*specify*] and your brand [*specify*] against competitors [*specify*].

GEN AI CO-PILOT IN ACTION
Leveraging Synthetic Customers

The product team of a large bank has leveraged gen AI to create synthetic customer segments capable of emulating human behavior.

Using AI-generated synthetic customer data, the team has tested responses to new products and services, as well as features that customers may desire most. This proved particularly useful in situations where traditional methods fell short or customer research was difficult to collect (such as during vulnerable situations like natural disasters, scams, or a loss in the family).

(Continued)

> By drawing on synthetic data, gen AI has helped the product team understand how customers might respond to changing contexts or unexpected financial challenges in a realistic environment. This informed the bank's product innovation process.

Synthetic research can be applied in various domains, for example, market research and data analysis, software testing (mainly to identify errors and shortcomings), and product development and testing. Synthetic data research can, however, go much deeper. Some areas of application require significant computational resources and computer power, as well as advanced skills and knowledge that not every manager may have. For example, AI can create a vast array of speech examples needed to train speech recognition models. Or it can create thousands of synthetic fraud cases to enhance the performance of AI models designed to detect fraud.

Regardless of your expertise, as a manager you need to be aware of the opportunities offered by synthetic research, as well as the inherent risks of using the generated data in your daily work, including the potential for inaccuracy, biases, and other ethical implications.

This chapter and the previous one explained how you can leverage gen AI as a Co-Pilot for data analysis and customer insights. These tasks can be valuable inputs or preparatory work to business case development or strategic decisions, which you will discover in the next chapter.

RECAP

For customer insights, using gen AI as a Co-Pilot can help you:

- Improve the efficiency of research design, such as survey creation, and analysis of customer feedback data.

- Produce synthetic data that mimics the characteristics of real customers or users.

CHAPTER 18

Gen AI for Business Case Development

This chapter covers three Co-Thinker tasks using gen AI for managing your business: **stakeholder perspectives**, **evaluating trade-offs**, and **risk identification and mitigation**.

Combined, these tasks are critical components in the construction of every business case. A persuasive business case tells a convincing story about a specific problem to solve (the business need), identifies impacted parties, and proposes a viable solution.

In today's volatile, uncertain, complex, and ambiguous (VUCA) business landscape, it is increasingly challenging to craft a compelling business case.[1] First, you need to understand the diverse perspectives of stakeholders, including shareholders, customers, employees, and regulators. Second, you need to carefully evaluate trade-offs between many business priorities, ranging from innovation to environmental responsibility. Finally, you need to manage and mitigate risks such as market volatility, regulatory changes, and technological advancements.

Using gen AI as a Co-Thinker can help you reflect on diverse stakeholder perspectives, assess difficult trade-offs, and evaluate and mitigate risks to ensure that your business case is resilient in a VUCA world.

Stakeholder Perspectives

Stakeholder perspectives are critical to building an effective business case. Yet managers may overlook (or not have time to consider) the views and needs of all stakeholders when dealing with complex business issues such as sustainability, digital transformation, or mergers and acquisitions. Taking the perspectives of all stakeholders can ensure that their concerns are considered in decision-making.[2]

Gen AI excels at assuming various roles and uncovering perspectives that may go unnoticed. By asking it to emulate different stakeholders, it helps you gain a more complete understanding of the ecosystem. This will enable you to take a more comprehensive and informed approach to complex challenges, ultimately improving collaborative initiatives and decision-making.

CO-THINKING DIALOGUE
Stakeholder Perspectives

Co-Thinker's role. Gen AI acts as an expert of systems thinking in collaborative innovation, capable of taking the perspective of multiple stakeholders (for example, circularity in a supply chain).

Setting. The setting for the dialogue is a one-to-one interaction between the manager and gen AI. After completing the dialogue with AI, the manager should continue the reflection and conversation offline to gather feedback from real stakeholders.

Dialogue outline

[*Step 1*] Gen AI asks the manager to share the problem and the list of external stakeholders that need to be involved, as the company alone cannot tackle it.

[*Step 2*] Gen AI suggests three other stakeholders that may have been overlooked. The manager provides feedback and validates the revised list of stakeholders.

[*Step 3*] Gen AI creates a table with these four columns: stakeholders, their specific needs, unresolved pain points, and associated root causes. Gen AI seeks feedback from the manager and incorporates it as necessary.

[*Step 4*] Gen AI asks the manager to select the three most critical stakeholders. Then, it suggests

(Continued)

177

three red flags and mitigation actions for the selected stakeholders. The manager provides feedback, review, and validation.

[*Step 5*] Gen AI suggests three immediate next
steps to initiate engagement with each selected
stakeholder in the field.

Create the prompt. Visit hbr.org/book-resources to
download an editable version of this dialogue outline.
Make any changes you wish and then copy and paste it
into a chatbot of your choosing.

Evaluating Trade-Offs

Almost every business decision involves difficult choices.
These decisions often require you to give up something
to gain something else. Win-win solutions aren't always
possible. In these situations, you must make trade-offs
and explain them to stakeholders. This is not an easy
process because it depends on multiple criteria, such as
money, the time horizon, and the need to balance the
various interests of your company or unit.

Gen AI as a Co-Thinker can help you effectively navigate this complexity, from evaluating alternatives to persuasively communicating decisions:

- **Ponder various criteria.** Before making a decision, *you can ask gen AI* to help you evaluate
  the pros and cons of different options. Gen AI
  can also suggest potential trade-offs between

various criteria, such as short term versus long term, quality versus speed, or innovation versus efficiency.

- **Try this:** Ask gen AI to help you consider the pros and cons of developing a new technology product [*specify*] in-house versus partnering with an external tech company.

- **Try this:** Ask gen AI to help you ponder the trade-offs between the transition toward eco-friendly packaging [*specify*] and traditional packaging [*specify*], based on factors such as [*specify, e.g., cost, shelf life, customer preferences, durability*].

- **Articulate the decision's rationale.** When you make a decision, you will usually need to communicate your choice to others such as your team, superiors, partners, or customers. In preparation for these conversations, *you can ask gen AI* to help you clarify and articulate how and why you made a particular decision. Effectively explaining the rationale when making trade-offs is critical to ensuring that stakeholders understand your purpose.[3]

  - **Try this:** Ask gen AI to break down your rationale [*specify*] into three clear, understandable points.

  - **Try this:** Ask gen AI to help you articulate the rationale [*specify*] as it relates to the company's purpose.

   – **Try this:** Ask gen AI to help you formulate clear, concise responses to likely questions that others will have about your decision [*specify*].

CO-THINKING DIALOGUE
Evaluating Trade-Offs

Co-Thinker's role. Gen AI acts as an expert in complex business decision-making.

Setting. The setting for the dialogue is a one-to-one interaction between the manager and gen AI.

Dialogue outline

[*Step 1*] Gen AI asks the manager to share information about the difficult decision and the solution options under consideration. Gen AI elaborates on it.

[*Step 2*] Gen AI asks the manager to explain the advantages and disadvantages of each solution option. Gen AI elaborates and integrates with additional pros and cons that may have been overlooked. The manager provides feedback.

[*Step 3*] Gen AI summarizes in a table the pros and cons for each solution option.

[*Step 4*] Gen AI suggests the two most relevant trade-offs based on the table. The manager comments and selects one. Then, gen AI simulates what might happen in different scenarios (potential impacts and implications).

[*Step 5*] Gen AI suggests three questions and related investigation activities to further evaluate the trade-off.

Create the prompt. Visit hbr.org/book-resources to download an editable version of this dialogue outline. Make any changes you wish and then copy and paste it into a chatbot of your choosing.

Risk Identification and Mitigation

With many industries considering their VUCA environment, almost every strategic initiative faces multiple risks that leaders must address to ensure success. By proactively mapping risks across potential business ventures, leaders can anticipate any vulnerabilities.

Generative AI as a Co-Thinker can help you identify and mitigate risk in various ways:

- **Risk mapping and evaluation.** *You can ask gen AI* to help you consider a long list of risks after sharing information about the difficult situation that you are facing (whether a market shift or an environmental challenge). You can then select certain risks for further analysis and ask gen AI to simulate risk variation under different conditions through examples and suggestions on implications. Once the mapping is complete, gen AI can also summarize the discussion, suggest mitigation strategies, and visualize the assessment results in a risk matrix (for example, "Guide me in creating a risk matrix by categorizing identified risks according to their likelihood of occurrence and potential impact").

- **De-risking projects.** If assumptions about your project go unchallenged, they can pose a significant risk to its success. *You can ask gen AI to help you reflect on the most critical assumptions by challenging and refining them, suggesting overlooked or hidden ones, and providing approaches for validation* (for example, a controlled experiment or simulation).

CO-THINKING DIALOGUE
Risk Identification and Mitigation

Co-Thinker's role. Gen AI acts as an expert in innovation management, applying frameworks such as Rita McGrath and Ian MacMillan's "discovery-driven planning," an approach for de-risking high-uncertainty projects and learning from potential mistakes as inexpensively and as early as possible.[a]

Setting. The setting for the dialogue can be one-to-one, with the manager and gen AI engaging in dialogue, or one-to-many, in a group setting where other team members join the manager. This arrangement allows more pauses for group reflection before returning to the dialogue with gen AI in the sequenced conversation.

Dialogue outline

[*Step 1*] Gen AI asks the manager to provide the project background and an initial list of assumptions. Gen AI revises this list, uncovering hidden assumptions and proposing additional ones that the manager may have overlooked in the preliminary list. The manager then provides feedback on these revisions.

[*Step 2*] Gen AI fine-tunes the list, adding or dropping assumptions from the checklist based on the manager's feedback and confirmation.

[*Step 3*] Gen AI proposes three criteria to prioritize the most critical assumptions that need to be tested first. The manager provides feedback on the proposed criteria.

[*Step 4*] Gen AI proposes actions for validation of each of the three most critical assumptions. The manager provides feedback on these proposed actions and requests further details.

[*Step 5*] Gen AI summarizes it into a validation plan—detailing which assumptions to test, in what sequence, and how. The manager then provides feedback, including modifications or additions, and confirms the plan.

[*Step 6*] Gen AI explains how it can concretely help the manager validate the selected assumptions.

(Continued)

Based on the validation of assumptions, the manager can return to the checklist [*Step 2*] to revise or pivot iteratively as new knowledge and insights on the assumptions emerge (either proving or disproving them).

Create the prompt. Visit hbr.org/book-resources to download an editable version of this dialogue outline. Make any changes you wish and then copy and paste it into a chatbot of your choosing.

a. Amy Gallo, "A Refresher on Discovery-Driven Planning," hbr.org, February 13, 2017, https://hbr.org/2017/02/a-refresher-on-discovery-driven-planning.

- **Simulating scenarios.** *You can ask gen AI* to run multiple scenarios and simulations. For example, you can ask, "Help me explore three 'What if' scenarios to stress-test my key assumptions [*specify*]." This is especially important when certain assumptions are critical to the success of the case (if these assumptions are disproven or found to be lacking, it could jeopardize the entire case). By using gen AI for such simulations, you can gain deeper insights into potential outcomes. This process not only helps you identify potential weaknesses but also helps you consider alternative strategies and modify your initial hypotheses, prepare for various contingencies, and make more-informed decisions.

Now that you have discussed with gen AI the opportunities, the risks, and the key stakeholders' perspectives on the solution option you're considering, you have all the needed insights and information to start developing your business case.

In this chapter, we have covered how gen AI as a Co-Thinker can support you in enhancing the strategic thinking capability you need to develop solid business cases. Now let's move on to how it can help you further with strategic decision-making.

RECAP

For developing a sound business case, using gen AI as a Co-Thinker can help you:

- Understand the perspectives, needs, and concerns of stakeholders.

- Navigate the complexity of trade-off evaluations, from assessing alternatives to communicating decisions in a compelling way.

- Consider the various risks and then mitigate them by reflecting on critical assumptions and testing them through simulations of different scenarios.

NOTES

1. Warren G. Bennis and Burt Nanus, *Leaders: Strategies for Taking Charge* (New York: Harper Collins, 1997).
2. Gabriele Rosani and Mattia Vettorello, "Seeing the Whole Picture," IMD, October 18, 2023, https://www.imd.org/ibyimd/strategy/seeing-the-whole-picture-why-perspective-taking-is-a-powerful-tool-for-sustainable-decision-making/.
3. Ranjay Gulati, "The Messy but Essential Pursuit of Purpose," *Harvard Business Review*, March–April 2022, https://hbr.org/2022/03/the-messy-but-essential-pursuit-of-purpose.

CHAPTER 19

Gen AI for Strategic Decisions

This chapter covers three Co-Thinker tasks using gen AI for managing your business: **formulating business strategy**, **evaluating innovative concepts**, and **assessing supply chain strategy**.

If you are a new or mid-level manager, strategy formulation may not be part of your job. However, as you move higher in the organization, you are expected to think strategically about your business and make deliberate choices that align well with your company's strategy. To do so effectively, you must ask higher-order questions, consider the implications of each course of action, and challenge common assumptions or beliefs.

Using generative AI as a Co-Thinker helps you hone your ability to think strategically and supports you in formulating or challenging your own team's or unit's strategy.

Formulating Business Strategy

Whether you are innovating your business model or creating a new business unit, you must evaluate opportunities such as new markets, geographies, product or service offerings, and threats to your business and your ability to respond. Your strategy should explain how your business will outperform competitors and secure its position. This involves mapping out the capabilities your organization needs to develop and the management systems required to support these ambitions. The approach you take to this analysis is important. If you treat it as a mere exercise, it will only be a plan. True strategy delves deeper. It's about making purposeful choices—selecting certain paths while intentionally forgoing others—and understanding the unique value you will offer to stand out in the competitive landscape.[1]

Leveraging gen AI as a Co-Thinker can guide you in the process of formulating your business strategy. *You can ask gen AI* to act as a methodology expert, helping to structure your thinking, enhancing your ideas, surfacing elements you may not have considered, and reflecting on capabilities that can support or constrain your strategy.

CO-THINKING DIALOGUE
Formulating Business Strategy

Co-Thinker's role. Gen AI acts as an expert of strategy formulation, applying frameworks such as Roger L. Martin's "five questions framework."[a]

Setting. The dialogue's setting primarily involves one-to-one interactions between the manager and gen AI. However, in the final step, gen AI suggests sharing the strategic-thinking conversation with other colleagues to gather additional perspectives and challenge strategic assumptions made during the various steps. Gen AI also advises the manager to reconvene and iteratively restart the conversation after incorporating feedback.

Dialogue outline

[*Step 1*] Gen AI asks the manager to outline the business strategy and its broader goal. Then, gen AI assists in elaborating on what success might look like and how to measure it in terms of key achievements.

[*Step 2*] Gen AI aids the manager in reflecting on the playing field (where to play) by posing questions such as: "Where are the most promising opportunities for your company in this market?" "Which sectors and segments are the most attractive, and why?" Gen AI can further articulate and enrich the manager's answers and may suggest additional opportunities that the manager might have missed.

[*Step 3*] Gen AI asks the manager to provide input about the main competitors, their strategy, and their offerings. Gen AI helps define the potential ingredients for a differentiating value proposition to win against other players (how to win). It can

(Continued)

189

also suggest alternative perspectives, patterns, or analogies to spark strategic creativity and value innovation. The manager gives feedback.

[*Step 4*] Gen AI suggests some capabilities to consider (such as assets, expertise, talent, knowledge, market access, network, and so on) and discusses with the manager their critical role in making the chosen strategy executable, based on the provided company context. Should the necessary capabilities for strategy execution be absent or too difficult to develop, gen AI can assist the manager in reevaluating the "where to play" and "how to win," thus iterating the reflection process.

[*Step 5*] Gen AI then assists in evaluating the systems, structures, and measures necessary to sustain and maintain the capabilities that enable the chosen strategy. Gen AI also helps reflect on the potential barriers and risks to be mitigated. The manager provides contextual insights into the company systems and their ability to support strategy implementation or their need for revision.

[*Step 6*] Gen AI summarizes the entire conversation into a table with five columns—winning aspiration, where to play, how to win, capabilities, and system—and outlines the recommended path forward to make the strategy actionable. The manager shares final feedback and comments.

Create the prompt: Visit hbr.org/book-resources to download an editable version of this dialogue outline. Make any changes you wish and then copy and paste it into a chatbot of your choosing.

a. Roger L. Martin, "Five Questions to Build a Strategy," hbr.org, May 26, 2010, https://hbr.org/2010/05/the-five-questions-of-strategy.

In addition to its role as a methodology expert, you can ask gen AI to actively engage in the discussion about a specific strategic challenge you are facing.[2] Pairing your team with a virtual strategist can help you experiment and innovate more.

Multi-Agent Strategy Discussion

In addition to problem-solving (see chapter 14, "Gen AI for Complex Problem-Solving"), multi-agent systems, which are a group of intelligent agents that can interact, communicate, share information, and work together, open up fascinating possibilities for strategy discussions.

Consider, for example, simulating a C-suite discussion about the company's plan to enter a new market segment. Each AI agent, with its unique expertise and capabilities, represents a specific profile (which could be anybody from an executive to an expert to external stakeholders) and contributes to the strategic

(Continued)

discussion with specialized knowledge and insights, challenges assumptions, and proposes solutions.

Using AI agents in strategy discussions can:

- Enrich the discussion with a diversity of viewpoints.

- Help anticipate potential concerns and help identify conflicts and trade-offs early in the strategy formulation process.

- Have conversations on strategy topics that managers may not be comfortable discussing directly with the C-suite executives or when other executives are unavailable.

- Help prepare for a persuasive strategy pitch or presentation by simulating potential reactions, objections, and questions.

Remember that while AI can be a valuable thought partner, the ultimate decision about business strategy is yours and your team's.

Evaluating Innovative Concepts

Continuous innovation is the key to growth. As a manager, you're aware of the necessity to innovate, but you also need to maintain discipline and rigor in managing the innovation portfolio and funnel to optimize limited resources. It's important to have a systematic process for evaluating new concepts (product, service, or solution) before making decisions and investments.

You can ask gen AI to help you and your team reflect on a set of key questions about the innovative concept. Gen AI facilitates your team's discussion by helping to articulate answers, finding supporting evidence, or playing devil's advocate by pointing out weaknesses and missing elements.

CO-THINKING DIALOGUE
Evaluating Innovative Concepts

Co-Thinker's role. Gen AI acts as an expert of innovation management, applying well-stablished frameworks for screening innovative concepts, such as George Day's "Is it real? Can we win? Is it worth doing?"[a]

Setting. The setting for the dialogue is a one-to-many interaction the manager conducts with their team, preferably cross-functional (including R&D, marketing, and manufacturing).

Dialogue outline

[*Step 1*] Gen AI asks the manager to share relevant content about the innovative concept to evaluate and asks specific questions to improve the level of understanding. The manager answers and provides further details.

[*Step 2*] Gen AI initiates the methodological discussion by posing a set of questions regarding the market attractiveness of the concept ("Is it real?"). For instance, it considers such questions as "Is there

(Continued)

---

a need or desire for the product?" and "Is the size of the potential market adequate?" Gen AI then challenges the manager's answers in a constructive way. For example, it can highlight points that need to be substantiated with more market evidence or customer feedback, rather than relying solely on opinions.

[*Step 3*] Gen AI assists the manager and the team in evaluating the competitive environment ("Can we win?"). It asks key questions: "Can a competitor's offering deliver the same results or benefits to customers?" "Is the advantage sustainable?" "How will competitors respond?" Gen AI takes on the role and perspective of competitors and simulates possible counteractions. The manager comments and provides feedback.

[*Step 4*] Gen AI helps the manager examine the risks versus payoffs ("Is it worth doing?"). It asks: "Will it cannibalize or improve sales of the company's existing products or services?" "Will it enhance or harm relationships with dealers, distributors, regulators, and so on?" Then, gen AI articulates scenarios to make the discussion more situational and realistic with a "what if" analysis.

[*Step 5*] Gen AI summarizes the main points of the discussion by structuring a table that lists the key dimensions, the corresponding questions addressed, and the answers provided. In addition,

gen AI lists questions where the answers were uncertain and suggests actions for gathering supporting evidence.

Create the prompt. Visit hbr.org/book-resources to
download an editable version of this dialogue outline.
Make any changes you wish and then copy and paste it
into a chatbot of your choosing.

a. George S. Day, "Is It Real? Can We Win? Is It Worth Doing?,"
Harvard Business Review, December 2007, https://hbr.org/2007/12/is-
it-real-can-we-win-is-it-worth-doing-managing-risk-and-reward-
in-an-innovation-portfolio.

Assessing Supply Chain Strategy

Numerous challenges span the entire spectrum of supply
chain operations: from ensuring supply chain resiliency
and sustainability to deciding on sourcing and produc-
tion strategies, navigating supplier selection choices,
and optimizing logistics strategies. The stakes are always
high, as these decisions not only have immediate operational impact, but also have long-term implications for
your business's competitiveness, financial health, and
brand reputation.

Navigating different options isn't straightforward.
Each decision encompasses multiple dimensions and
has potential effects on various business aspects.[3] Consider these examples:

- Diversifying your supplier base to bolster supply chain resilience could increase operational

complexity and cost, challenging the lean operating principles many businesses favor.

- Onshoring and nearshoring can improve supply chain resilience and sustainability but could lead to higher costs.

- Outsourcing, while lower cost, could introduce vulnerabilities to resilience and agility amid global uncertainties such as trade tensions and pandemics.

- Implementing buffer stocks and redundancies deviates from just-in-time inventory norms and brings greater costs but is important to reduce supply chain disruptions.

Using gen AI as a Co-Thinker can help you reflect on various areas of your supply chain strategy:

- **Supply sources diversification.** *You can ask gen AI* to converse about different factors such as geographic risk, supplier reliability, cost variability, and complexity of logistics. In the dialogue, request that gen AI share examples or simulate real-world scenarios. For example, "Imagine you are a company [*specify*] evaluating two different supply chain strategies. You are torn between maintaining a lean approach with fewer preferred suppliers or diversifying your network [*specify*]. Given these considerations, describe the factors you should weigh when making the decision."

TIP
How to Engage with Gen AI on Supply Chain Management

When you are discussing supply chain management with gen AI, try the following questions, requesting articulation and examples that fit your case. Always share details about your context that can enrich the conversation:

Cost versus quality. "How do organizations typically balance the pursuit of lower costs without compromising the quality of materials or services from suppliers?"

Single-source versus multiple suppliers. "What are the common trade-offs between relying on a single supplier for cost efficiency and integration versus diversifying suppliers for increased resilience?"

Long-term contracts versus flexibility. "What are the pros and cons of committing to long-term contracts to ensure supply stability and favorable terms versus prioritizing flexibility to adapt to market changes more readily?"

Local versus global suppliers. "What aspects should we consider when weighing the benefits of local suppliers for shorter lead times and sustainability against the potential cost savings or unique offerings of global suppliers?"

(Continued)

> **Collaboration versus competition.** "In managing our supplier relationships, what are the trade-offs between fostering collaboration for innovation and efficiency versus maintaining a competitive approach for cost savings?"

- **Location strategy.** *You can ask gen AI* to discuss your logistics and manufacturing location strategy by considering key factors such as labor costs, market access, regulatory environments, and geopolitical stability across different regions. By sharing examples from your industry and others, gen AI can help you ponder various strategies (reshoring, friendshoring, nearshoring, offshoring) that can enhance supply chain security and responsiveness.

- **Technological disruptions.** *You can ask gen AI* to help you reflect on how new technologies may impact your industry supply chain and operations.[4] You can start a conversation based on this input and deep dive on a specific new technology and learn about its potential applications in your industry.

In this section, we have described how gen AI can assist you in managing your business, serving as a Co-Pilot for tasks such as data analysis and customer insights, or as a Co-Thinker for more complex tasks including business case development and strategic decision-making. Now, let's proceed to section five, which focuses on managing change with gen AI.

RECAP

For strategic decision-making, using gen AI as a Co-Thinker can help you:

- Formulate or challenge your business strategy based on popular frameworks.

- Evaluate innovative concepts before making decisions and investments.

- Assess your supply chain strategy in terms of sources, locations, and technologies.

NOTES

1. Roger Martin, *The Difference Between a Plan and a Strategy* (podcast), hbr.org, May 26, 2023.

2. Michael Olenick and Peter Zemsky, "Can GenAI Do Strategy?," hbr.org, November 24, 2023, https://hbr.org/2023/11/can-genai-do -strategy.

3. Willy C. Shih, "Global Supply Chains in a Post-Pandemic World," *Harvard Business Review*, September–October 2020, https:// hbr.org/2020/09/global-supply-chains-in-a-post-pandemic-world.

4. Narendra Agrawal et al., "How Machine Learning Will Transform Supply Chain Management," *Harvard Business Review*, March– April 2024, https://hbr.org/2024/03/how-machine-learning-will -transform-supply-chain-management.

Managing Change with Generative AI

CHAPTER 20

Change Management Tasks That Are Enhanced with Gen AI

Every manager knows the challenges of introducing change to their teams, whether it entails a new system, a revised process, a new way of working, or a shift in the business model. Depending on the context, employees' reactions to change may be passive or more outspoken. Even if there isn't outright resistance, it's common to hear complaints like "Don't they know this is not a good time?" or "Yet another change to deal with."[1]

Change is difficult, both for employees and for the managers who must lead by example. Depending on your role in the organization, your involvement in

TABLE 20-1

Change management tasks enhanced with gen AI

	Co-Pilot	Co-Thinker
Managing change	**Transformation support** • Planning and monitoring • Communication and engagement	**Leading change** • Defining the transformation strategy • Overcoming resistance • Promoting a mindset shift

change management may vary. If you are an HR manager, your focus might be on the people side, ensuring that employees are informed, supported, and equipped with the necessary training to adapt to new processes or systems. If you are a business unit manager, your objective is to align the change strategy with business goals, manage the impact on your unit's operations, and guide your team through the transformation.

Technology and data can significantly increase the odds of effective change initiatives. According to Capgemini Invent's research, managers who implement data-driven change are more successful than those who do not leverage data.[2] Generative AI can be particularly helpful to drive change management efforts along the entire transformation journey.

As a Co-Pilot, gen AI can assist you with the operational tasks of change management such as planning (defining the structure and sequence of phases and activities of a change initiative), communicating (tailoring content and channels to different groups within the organization), and monitoring (real-time tracking and analysis of engagement levels).

As a Co-Thinker, gen AI helps you with more complex tasks. First, it can act as a change management expert, guiding you in the selection and implementation of the most appropriate approach for your specific situation. It can help you ponder strategic choices, such as the speed and the scope of the change, and the degree of involvement of stakeholders. Second, it can help you reflect on the types of resistance you are experiencing or anticipating, ask you about the causes, and assist you in skillfully applying methods for dealing with it. Finally, gen AI can be your thought partner as you reflect on how to promote the mindset shifts necessary to keep the momentum of change going.

In this section, you will learn how to practice gen AI as a Co-Pilot for transformation support (chapter 21) with concrete examples of prompts that you can try. In addition, you will learn how to use gen AI as a Co-Thinker for leading change (chapter 22) with all the instructions to build your Co-Thinking dialogues for a value-added conversation with gen AI and to transform your outlines into immediately executable prompts.

RECAP

Gen AI can enhance change management in both Co-Pilot mode (for transformation support) and Co-Thinker mode (for leading change).

- Using gen AI as a Co-Pilot can support operational tasks such as planning, communicating, and monitoring of change management initiatives.

- Using gen AI as a Co-Thinker can help you reflect on the appropriate change management approach, anticipate, or deal with resistance, as well as promote new mindset shifts.

NOTES

1. Erika Andersen, "Change Is Hard. Here's How to Make It Less Painful," hbr.org, April 7, 2022, https://hbr.org/2022/04/change-is -hard-heres-how-to-make-it-less-painful.

2. Change Management Study 2023, Capgemini Invent, January 24, 2023, based on a survey of 1,175 managers.

CHAPTER 21

Gen AI for Transformation Support

This chapter covers two Co-Pilot tasks using gen AI to manage change: **planning and monitoring** and **communication and engagement**.

Perpetual transformation has become the norm. Organizations constantly evolve to adapt to technological innovations, meet sustainability goals, navigate geopolitical tensions, or respond to economic fluctuations. Within this context, transformation projects have taken center stage as companies embrace the change of their business and organization.[1]

Change can happen at different levels—company, division, unit, subunit, or even team levels. Some initiatives may be large scale and long term, such as digital transformations. Smaller but important change projects could involve, for example, a regional sales head putting into action a new selling approach that requires retraining salespeople, or a frontline manager tasked with implementing a new performance management system on their team. Nonetheless, while the scale may vary, the principles of effective change management apply universally across all levels and functions.

As a manager, you need to be prepared to lead change within your team or unit. Traditionally, this has entailed a considerable investment of time and resources, including necessary but often burdensome tasks such as reporting.

By using generative AI as a Co-Pilot, you can streamline numerous operational tasks related to change management such as planning, monitoring, and communication. This can free up your time to focus on the more challenging and critical aspects crucial for transformation success.

Planning and Monitoring

Change initiatives, especially large ones, often require a significant amount of administrative work to maintain up-to-date information about ongoing programs. Generative AI can alleviate this reporting burden and offer new enhancements as well.[2] Using gen AI as a Co-Pilot can alleviate and optimize project management tasks related to managing change:

- **Change task force setup.** *You can ask gen AI* to suggest the optimal team composition (for example, "Based on best practices in similar change initiatives, are there any skills or profiles missing from my project charter?") and then draft a document detailing who does what to avoid role conflicts and ambiguity.

- **Try this:** Ask gen AI to provide a detailed breakdown of the key responsibilities and necessary skills required for a change champion role within department [*specify*]. Then, ask gen AI to include two specific support activities the champion should prioritize in each phase of the transformation [*specify*].

- **Try this:** Ask gen AI to create a draft team charter for a change initiative [*specify*] based on the notes you provide [*share, link, or upload*].

• **Program planning.** *You can ask gen AI* to detail the various streams of the change initiative and to identify any dependencies, synergies, and touch-points between the streams. If you already have a plan in the form of a document or presentation, you can ask gen AI for feedback on the structure of streams (for example, "Are there any missing streams?"), sequence of streams (for example, "Are there any potential bottlenecks?"), or description of streams (for example, "Are there any potential ambiguities in the way streams are described?").

• **Stakeholder updates.** *You can ask gen AI* to help you organize a stakeholder meeting (for example, "Create a 45-minute agenda for a recurring update meeting with stakeholder [*specify*]"), prepare content (for example, "Extract three key messages from the latest program update document and tailor them for stakeholder [*specify*]"), and debrief (for example, "Summarize questions raised by the stakeholder [*specify*] about the change program and list the key points I need to clarify before the next update call").

- **Performance monitoring.** *You can ask gen AI to* help you define the appropriate metrics that are closely aligned with the transformation goals, as well as to suggest ways to communicate them in an effective way.[3]

  - **Try this:** Ask gen AI to provide a list of 10 common metrics for the change management program [*specify*].

  - **Try this:** Ask gen AI to suggest three ways to visualize employee engagement levels as measured by [*specify the metric*].

GEN AI CO-PILOT FOR MEASURING CHANGE

Identify. Ask gen AI, "List five metrics for workstream [*specify*]." Specify the type or format and provide examples of what a good metric looks like.

Formulate. Ask gen AI, "For each metric, recommend two key performance indicators and the related formula."

Measure. Ask gen AI, "For each metric, verify data availability in document [*specify*] or database [*specify*]."

Interpret. Ask gen AI, "In the data set [*share, link, or upload*], list outliers by metric and suggest potential explanation, for example, error or trend to consider."

Communicate. Ask gen AI, "Translate metric [*specify*] into a short textual message and visual for stakeholder [*specify*]."

- **Customized reporting.** *You can ask gen AI to create customized reports for different stakeholders, adapting the format, style, and messages. For instance, it can generate executive summaries for senior management, detailed progress reports for project teams, or visual dashboards for internal communication.*

  - **Try this:** Ask gen AI to provide a summary of the current status of the workstream [*share, link, or upload*] for the upcoming program steering committee meeting. Focus on three key areas: progress (stream KPIs), explanation of gaps (versus targets), and mitigation actions.

  - **Try this:** Ask gen AI to create a report based on the document [*share, link, or upload*] focusing on selected metrics [*specify*] over the last quarter.

- **Learning capture.** If gen AI is integrated into your company's knowledge management systems, *you can ask gen AI* to articulate collected lessons, best practices, and success stories, facilitating knowledge capture and transfer across the organization.

  - **Try this:** Ask gen AI to analyze the project reports [*share, link, or upload*] and summarize key lessons learned.

  - **Try this:** Ask gen AI to analyze feedback from employees [*share, link, or upload*] and identify areas for improvement.

  - **Try this:** Ask gen AI to create an engaging narrative around the success stories [*share, link, or upload*].

  - **Try this:** Ask gen AI to create a weekly digest with early wins based on document [*share, link, or upload*] that could benefit other teams and accelerate change.

Communication and Engagement

Effective communication and engagement are essential to the success of any change project. Traditionally, these tasks have been resource-intensive, requiring significant time and effort to prepare content, messages, and materials, and to organize events addressing diverse audiences. Now, managers can use generative AI as a Co-Pilot to streamline and enhance the operational aspects of communication and engagement.

- **Customized communication.** *You can ask gen AI* to draft communication materials (for example, emails, newsletters, announcements) tailored to different stakeholder groups. For instance, "In the newsletter for audience [*specify*] in unit [*specify*], suggest three references to relevant documents, videos, or internal articles." Moreover, for organizations undergoing transformation across different countries, you can ask gen AI to translate communications into local languages, promoting better comprehension of transformation initiatives.

TIP

Data-Driven Storytelling with Gen AI

Harnessing supporting data is important for effective change communication. It can enrich the storytelling process and enhance the credibility of your message to increase acceptance and buy-in throughout the transformation.

Try these: Once you have shared with gen AI the main goals of your change management initiative, you can ask:

- **Evidence "for" change.** "Access document [*specify*] or database [*specify*] and extract key data to support the reason for the change considering the context of unit, team, or country [*specify*]."

(Continued)

- **Evidence "of" change.** "Draft a narrative about the success story of team [*specify*] including quantitative data on key achievements [*specify data sources, for example, folder, database, chat, or email thread*]."

- **Customized engagement.** *You can ask gen AI to* apply gamification principles and design interactive challenges or quizzes related to transformation goals.[4] By incorporating elements of competition, rewards, and progression, gamified experiences motivate stakeholders to actively participate in the transformation journey, fostering camaraderie and teamwork.

  - **Try this:** Ask gen AI to design a role-playing game where [*target audience*] navigates through scenarios related to the change, making decisions and experiencing the outcomes of those choices.

  - **Try this:** Ask gen AI to recommend three multiple-choice quizzes suitable for [*target audience*] based on the learning objectives covered in the training material [*link, share, or upload document*]. The quizzes should focus on assessing participants' understanding of key transformation concepts and their application to real-world scenarios.

GEN AI CO-PILOT IN ACTION
Leveraging Gamification

As part of a large company's sustainability transformation program, the change management team leveraged gen AI to create the "sustainability champions challenge," an engaging and personalized training initiative.

Gen AI generated interactive quizzes and activities focused on reducing carbon emissions, providing employees with tailored questions. For instance, engineers received questions on optimizing energy usage in their departments, while marketing professionals tackled challenges related to promoting sustainable product packaging.

Moreover, gen AI automated the entire game loop for each individual, adjusting difficulty levels and evolving content to maintain engagement. Employees with consistently high scores received more difficult questions, while those needing additional support received targeted learning resources.

By gamifying the learning experience with gen AI's assistance, the company not only facilitated knowledge transfer but also encouraged adoption of sustainable behaviors.

- **Question and answer creation.** *You can ask gen AI* to create questions and answers (Q&A) from a document that you share, link, or upload. Gen AI can suggest a series of Q&A pairs that address concerns and doubts, and provide practical information, examples, or links to sections of the document for further reading. Then you can decide on the format and style, check for accuracy, and validate content.

– **Try this:** Ask gen AI to create 10 Q&A pairs based on the document [*share, link, or upload*] and specify the type of answers you'd like to have (such as short answers of a few words, long answers that are two sentences, or true-or-false answers).

– **Try this:** Ask gen AI to create a troubleshooting guide for the change program [*specify*]. The guide should be organized as a series of Q&As, where each answer provides structured, step-by-step guidance and additional resources or tips.

This chapter explored how gen AI can support operational tasks for program management during change initiatives. In the next chapter, you'll discover how gen AI can be a strategic thought partner to address critical aspects of change management, such as overcoming resistance and fostering a mindset shift within your team.

RECAP

In transformation programs, using gen AI as a Co-Pilot can help you streamline and enhance operational tasks such as:

- Planning and monitoring change initiatives and assisting with project team design, stakeholder updates, reporting, and learning capture.

- Supporting your communication and engagement through custom messaging and gamification, and creating Q&As.

NOTES

1. Antonio Nieto-Rodriguez, "The Project Economy Has Arrived," *Harvard Business Review*, November–December 2021, https://hbr.org/2021/11/the-project-economy-has-arrived.

2. Antonio Nieto-Rodriguez and Ricardo Viana Vargas, "How AI Will Transform Project Management," hbr.org, February 2, 2023, https://hbr.org/2023/02/how-ai-will-transform-project-management.

3. Michael Schrage et al., "Improve Key Performance Indicators with AI," *MIT Sloan Management Review*, July 11, 2023, https://sloanreview.mit.edu/article/improve-key-performance-indicators-with-ai/.

4. "Does Gamified Training Get Results?" *Harvard Business Review*, March–April 2023, https://hbr.org/2023/03/does-gamified-training-get-results.

CHAPTER 22

Gen AI for Leading Change

This chapter covers three Co-Thinker tasks using gen AI for managing change: **defining the transformation strategy**, **overcoming resistance**, and **promoting a mindset shift**.

As a manager, you will inevitably find yourself in situations where leading change is a necessity. Whether change is needed for adjusting to shifts in customer preferences, adopting new technology tools within a department, reorganizing a unit after an acquisition, or restructuring a specific workflow, change is never easy. There are always obstacles and resistance to overcome. Successful change begins with you, as a manager, serving as a role model and helping your team embrace the necessary mindset shift for the desired changes.

Using gen AI as a Co-Thinker can be a powerful ally at multiple critical stages.

First, gen AI can help you explain the need for change and articulate a clear vision and strategy. *You can ask gen AI* to have a conversation on how to craft a compelling narrative around the "why" of change.

Second, gen AI can help you overcome resistance throughout the transformation journey. *You can ask gen AI* to help you reflect on potential objections and points of friction, debate with you about the root causes of the resistance, and converge on appropriate communication actions to address concerns and bring people along.

Ultimately, success depends on winning people's hearts and minds to ensure they fully embrace and internalize the change. *You can ask gen AI* to help you promote a mindset shift in your team by providing concrete examples and practical tips for translating the new mindset into specific actions and daily habits.

Defining the Transformation Strategy

Four factors are critical when defining the transformation: clarity on the reasons for change, a convincing message about the urgency of the change, a clear vision of the desired future state, and the approach to achieve it.

CO-THINKING DIALOGUE
Defining the Transformation Strategy

Co-Thinker's role. Gen AI acts as an expert in change management, applying best practices from the most authoritative theories, such as John Kotter's eight-step model.[a]

Setting. The dialogue setting primarily involves one-to-one interactions between the manager and gen AI. However, in the final step, the manager reviews the drafted vision and strategy articulation for the change with selected stakeholders.

Dialogue outline

[*Step 1*] Gen AI asks the manager to articulate why change is needed. The manager answers and provides contextual information.

[*Step 2*] Gen AI helps the manager identify the most relevant evidence (data, information) to convey the sense of urgency.

[*Step 3*] Gen AI asks the manager about areas of resistance. Then it provides a list of typical barriers to change and examples. The manager can provide more contextual information about the organizational barriers that exist in the firm so that gen AI can better tailor references to similar cases and how the barriers were removed.

[*Step 4*] Gen AI assists the manager in assessing key stakeholders for the transformation, reflecting

(Continued)

on their importance, and identifying the most critical ones to bring on board.

[*Step 5*] Gen AI drafts a compelling vision statement
to inspire change. The manager reviews it.

[*Step 6*] Starting from the vision statement, gen AI articulates the main pillars of the transformation strategy. The manager comments and provides feedback.
Gen AI suggests gathering feedback from selected
stakeholders and reconvening for further iterations.

Create the prompt. Visit hbr.org/book-resources to
download an editable version of this dialogue outline.
Make any changes you wish and then copy and paste it
into a chatbot of your choosing.

a. John P. Kotter, Vanessa Akhtar, and Gaurav Gupta, *Change: How Organizations Achieve Hard-to-Imagine Results in Uncertain and Volatile
Times* (New York: Wiley, 2021).

Overcoming Resistance

Across industries and sectors, the history of implementing organizational change is disappointingly poor.
Research shows that between 50% and 75% of change
efforts fail.[1] And even among those that succeed, many
fall short of their original goals. Why is change so difficult? One of the primary obstacles to effective change
is people. This holds true at every level, whether within
the entire company, a single division, a subunit, or even
a smaller team. A central part of your responsibility as a
manager is to help individuals overcome the innate, very
human tendency to cling to the status quo.

Gen AI as a Co-Thinker can help you examine the reasons for resistance in your team and identify ways to overcome them.

- **Anticipate potential resistance.** *You can ask gen AI* to provide a list of typical sources of resistance and describe the common underlying psychological and organizational mechanisms that cause them. Remember to offer examples related to your specific situation so that gen AI can help you reflect on the reasons behind the resistance and help you to detect early signals.

- **Suggest practical ways to reduce resistance.** *You can ask gen AI* to guide you through a set of methodological questions, making it easier to find effective solutions for dealing with resistance. In this process, based on your specific resistance situation, gen AI can share examples of successful change management tactics, including case studies where managers overcame similar problems with proven mitigation strategies.

CO-THINKING DIALOGUE
Overcoming Resistance

Co-Thinker's role. Gen AI acts as an expert in change management.

Setting. The dialogue's setting primarily involves one-to-one interactions between the manager and gen AI.

(Continued)

Dialogue outline

[*Step 1*] Gen AI asks the manager to provide contextual input on the change program. The manager answers. Then gen AI illustrates the typical sources of resistance (such as Rosabeth Moss Kanter's 10 most common sources of resistance).[a] The manager provides feedback or asks for additional input.

[*Step 2*] Gen AI asks the manager to select the source of resistance that is most relevant to the current context.

[*Step 3*] Gen AI asks the manager three methodological questions to dive deeper into early signals or warnings of resistance.

[*Step 4*] Gen AI draws on literature and suggests two specific actions for dealing with the source of resistance.

Create the prompt. Visit hbr.org/book-resources to download an editable version of this dialogue outline. Make any changes you wish and then copy and paste it into a chatbot of your choosing.

a. Rosabeth Moss Kanter, "Ten Reasons People Resist Change," hbr.org, September 25, 2012, https://hbr.org/2012/09/ten-reasons-people-resist-chang.

Promoting a Mindset Shift

As a manager, you have an important role in helping others adopt a mindset shift to embrace change. Simply communicating the need for a new mindset and articulating it through written communication is not enough. If you don't follow up repeatedly, there's a good chance the essential mindset change won't happen.

Generative AI allows you to actively involve your team in experiences that immerse them in the rationale, benefits, and practical applications of the desired new mindset. This activation increases engagement, buy-in, and the durability of the mindset transformation you are striving to lead.

LEVERAGING GEN AI FOR MINDSET SHIFT AT A FINANCE DEPARTMENT

Amy is the head of finance at an organization that is becoming more globally integrated. She needs to promote a mindset shift within her department from a locally focused mentality to a global one. Despite conducting awareness sessions, distributing materials, and making presentations, Amy is concerned that her team may not truly be adopting the mindset in day-to-day operations.

To more actively drive the mindset shift, Amy asks all of her direct reports to use gen AI to think about the implications and benefits of adopting a global mindset in finance.

(Continued)

Amy's team members go through a well-guided Co-Thinking dialogue. Then Amy organizes a team meeting where each direct report shares their experience interacting with gen AI about adopting a global mindset.

Thanks to gen AI, what started as passive awareness of the global mindset transforms into an activated experience for Amy's finance team.

To promote and encourage practicing mindset shifts in everyday situations, gen AI can help you and your team in a structured manner. Starting from the desired mindset shift, team members engage in structured dialogue with gen AI, evaluating the mindset maturity, reflecting on areas for improvement, and receiving tailored suggestions and scenario examples.

CO-THINKING DIALOGUE
Promoting a Mindset Shift

Co-Thinker's role. Gen AI acts as an expert in mindset change, providing methodological coaching on what is needed and how it can be practiced concretely.

Setting. The dialogue's setting is a self-reflection between the team member and gen AI. In the final step, gen AI suggests that the team member rejoin the conversation after a few weeks of testing the new mindset's behaviors to discuss the progress or address potential challenges in the implementation. In this way, the reflection is the starting point of a learning journey through follow-up sessions.

Dialogue outline. Structured dialogue between each team member and gen AI.

[*Step 1*] Gen AI asks the team member to share contextual information about the organization, the new mindset to adopt, and the reason for the shift. Then it elaborates with examples or situational scenarios to clarify what the new mindset means in practice and how to embody it. The team member comments on the examples.

[*Step 2*] Gen AI asks the team member three questions to help evaluate the current maturity of the individual's mindset shift. The team member reflects on the results of this self-evaluation and prioritizes the areas of opportunity to reduce the gap versus the desired mindset.

[*Step 3*] Based on the selected areas of opportunity, gen AI asks the team member to share an example from daily work.

[*Step 4*] Gen AI suggests three good practices, tips, and routines that the team member can apply. The team member comments and selects one.

[*Step 5*] Gen AI recommends rejoining the dialogue after a few weeks to discuss any challenges that have arisen in implementing the selected practice.

(Continued)

> **Create the prompt.** Visit hbr.org/book-resources to download an editable version of this dialogue outline. Make any changes you wish and then copy and paste it into a chatbot of your choosing.

We have covered how gen AI can support you in leading change. We now conclude the exploration of 35 managerial tasks that gen AI can enhance. Finally, in the epilogue, we'll explore the impact of generative AI on ways of working and how you can prepare for the gen AI–enabled future.

RECAP

In leading change, using gen AI as a Co-Thinker can support you in driving important tasks such as:

- Articulating a clear need for change and a compelling vision.

- Understanding the reasons for resistance and how to overcome them.

- Helping your team embrace new mindsets required by the change.

NOTE

1. Sally Blount and Shana Carroll, *Overcome Resistance to Change with Two Conversations*, hbr.org, May 16, 2017, https://hbr.org/2017/05/overcome-resistance-to-change-with-two-conversations.

Beyond Tasks: Generative AI's Impact on Ways of Working

This book has shown you 35 ways to use gen AI in your work as a manager. We hope that you have tried out many of them and have explored additional tasks to help you in your own role. Now that you recognize the power of gen AI, your next goal should be empowering your employees to use the technology at scale. And whether you're managing a team or unit, or leading a company, it's not as simple as just telling people to start using gen AI.

Before you begin, you'll need to consider a few questions:

- How will generative AI reshape the operations of my team, unit, or function?

- Is it necessary to revise our traditional workflows and, if so, in what ways?

- What new skills are essential for us to acquire, and how?

- What new rules should we establish?

To address these questions effectively, it's crucial to follow a clear path that starts with experimentation, leads to learning and upskilling, and ultimately culminates in reimagining workflows where humans and machines work in synergy. This epilogue aims to guide you as you begin that journey.

A Four-Step Transformation Journey

Throughout the many examples in this book, you have seen how gen AI can collaborate with you in brainstorming ideas, analyzing data, guiding reflections, and offering suggestions. You and your team will need to become acquainted with this blended way of working with intelligent machines. You and your team will require new skills. New team dynamics will emerge. You will have to redesign workflows to incorporate the role of AI in various tasks and steps, ultimately leading to organizational changes.

Your transformation journey should include four steps:

1. **Experiment in both modes.** To begin, engage your team in structured experimentation with a selection of tasks, starting with noncritical workflows. It's important to work with both modes of interaction (Co-Pilot and Co-Thinker) to gain familiarity and understand what's required to collaborate effectively with gen AI.

2. **Build new skills.** Learn how to talk to gen AI, becoming skilled at prompting, and hone your and your team's conversational skills to shape human-AI dialogues. While you experiment, always emphasize human judgment and critical thinking to mitigate the risk of overreliance on the model.[1]

3. **Redesign workflows.** Rethink processes and related tasks in ways that foster human-AI collaboration. Decide who should be doing what (sometimes, you may want AI to execute with light oversight, while for other tasks, you may want the human to be in the driver's seat) and determine the appropriate sequence of collaboration.

4. **Establish collective responsibility.** Provide guidelines and frameworks to foster responsible and ethical use, ultimately promoting a culture of collective responsibility.

Let's examine all four steps in detail.

1. Experiment in Both Modes

In sections two through five, you learned how to use gen AI for various tasks and how to interact with it. When you're ready to expand these experiments from a small team to hundreds of people, figuring out where to start and how to do it is crucial. Too much freedom can lead to confusion and risky practices, while too much control can stifle creativity and learning. The key is to find a middle ground. We suggest experimenting with a mix of tasks through a phased approach. Remember to be disciplined in experimentation, keeping track of the benefits, risks, and lessons learned.

Your experimentation portfolio should include both modes: Co-Pilot and Co-Thinker. The Co-Pilot mode is best for large-scale experiments where gen AI streamlines tasks that many people perform, such as analyzing data or drafting slides. It's suited for tasks with a broad impact, making it ideal for experiments involving a lot of participants to measure whether and how gen AI can boost productivity. Meanwhile, the Co-Thinker mode is a better fit for specialized, tailored experiments. In this role, a group of experts collaborate with gen AI on complex tasks, such as solving a problem. They should design conversation outlines and test structured prompt sequences iteratively, engaging in dialogue with and ultimately cocreating the output with gen AI.

Also consider experimenting with combinations: design one task as a Co-Pilot that informs a subsequent task as a Co-Thinker (for example, data analysis informing strategy formulation). Or reverse the order (for example, reflecting on change management strategy and then creating tailored communications for a target group).

Begin by reviewing the table of common management tasks found in this guide. Discuss them with your team and identify the first set of tasks for igniting the experimentation.

HOW TO IDENTIFY TASKS FOR DISCIPLINED EXPERIMENTATION

You can discuss this list of suggested criteria with your team when prioritizing tasks for gen AI experimentation. Consider aspects of impact and feasibility for each task. Below are examples of criteria and dimensions to evaluate.

Impact

- **Business impact.** Assess the tangible benefits, both short (such as productivity or cost savings) and medium term (such as product innovation).

- **Functional fit.** Consider the task's relevance to the specific function or unit (such as customer research for marketing or speech preparation for public relations).

- **Learning.** Assess the potential for enhancing skill development (for example, prompting human-machine conversation).

(Continued)

Feasibility

- **Compliance.** Check that your company policies and regulations authorize the use of gen AI for the task at hand.

- **Access.** Check with your IT department on the availability of the appropriate technology and features for your experiment.

- **Risks.** Exclude tasks that are too risky, considering factors such as data privacy, regulatory restrictions, ethical concerns, output quality, and reliability.

- **Limitations.** Evaluate the obstacles for wider application in the organization that could hinder scalability.

As the discussion unfolds, plot all the tasks you consider on a 2x2 impact-feasibility matrix. Then, focus on the "high impact, high feasibility" quadrant for the selection.

There's no one-size-fits-all solution. The same tasks might be assessed differently by various departments or in distinct contexts. For instance, for an innovation department, tasks like customer insights and idea generation may be crucial, while content generation might hold more significance for the communications department.

Here is a sample case developed by a finance team:

FIGURE E-1

Sample impact/feasibility 2x2 for gen AI tasks

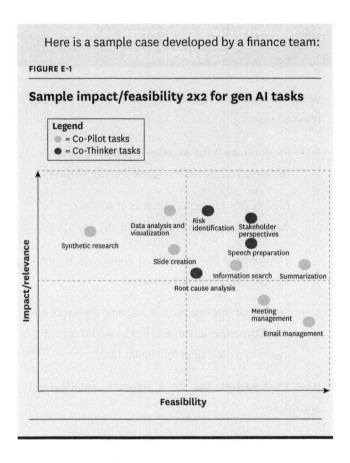

It can be beneficial to experiment in multiple rounds. You can adjust your experimentation plan based on your learnings before moving to the next round. Having a structured, phased approach to experimentation in place is also essential for a comprehensive evaluation of the benefits, risks, and barriers.

HOW TO HAVE A STRUCTURED APPROACH TO EXPERIMENTS

What to measure. Consider, for example, various dimensions:

- Productivity (time saved in a specific task or increased output in the same amount of time)

- Quality (for example, in terms of accuracy, depth, clarity, creativity, and so on)

- Engagement (for example, dropout rate, unused licenses, training participation)

- Sentiment (for example, if and how the users enjoyed the experience, and if they would recommend to a colleague for similar tasks)

How to measure. Set up a rigorous experimental approach:

- **Articulate tasks.** Describe tasks and subtasks clearly, outlining the expected output format and content to the testers.

- **Specify KPIs.** Define specific metrics to track for each task.

- **Control group.** Compare testers with a group that does not have access to gen AI.

- **Time-boxing.** Allocate the same amount of time to each group to complete a task.

- **Evaluation rubric.** Ensure that assessors maintain a consistent approach to scoring.

- **Outliers' interviews.** Focus on both the best and worst performers to better understand challenges and best practices.

- **Community of practice.** Listen to the real-time voice of the users on enterprise chat channels, sharing learnings, exchanging feedback, and so on.

After the first weeks of experimentation, organize a retrospective session with your team to discuss what is going well and what could be improved. Collect additional, more detailed learnings from the experiments.

Remember to consider trade-offs between metrics. In addition to analyzing metrics separately, it's crucial to view them holistically:

- **Speed versus quality.** While speed boosts efficiency, it may come at the cost of depth, accuracy, and clarity.

- **Individual use versus collaboration.** Boosting individual performance may hinder collective creativity and collaboration. Overreliance on machines can reduce team interaction.

- **Short-term gains versus long-term effects.** While cutting costs offers immediate

(Continued)

benefits, it can lead to long-term worker dissatisfaction and related negative consequences.[a]

a. Armin Granulo et al., "The Social Cost of Algorithmic Management," hbr.org, February 15, 2024, https://hbr.org/2024/02/the-social-cost-of-algorithmic-management.

2. Build New Skills

Experimentation will also help you understand which skills your team needs to develop most. Start where your testers encounter specific challenges or barriers in using gen AI. For instance, your team may find it challenging to effectively prompt gen AI to perform certain tasks or may struggle when crafting a suitable outline for a human-machine dialogue. Testers may encounter common pitfalls, such as placing too much trust in the machine, only to realize later that additional verification was indeed necessary.

Knowledge of prompting techniques, both basic (simple queries) and advanced (structured prompts), is an important skill, and it is likely where you should begin your upskilling efforts. Universities and learning vendors offer many online courses on prompting. Some enterprise gen AI tools are packaged with courses on how to use them. Many companies have also created "prompt academies" to train their employees, while offering a platform to share and collect learnings ("prompt libraries").

Prompting builds on human skills such as how to ask good questions, how to engage in an effective conversation, and how to exercise critical judgment.[2] Therefore, prompting per se is not enough. Some organizations make the mistake of investing in prompting only in their gen AI development—by contrast, they should invest continuously in more fundamental skills and competencies that make humans truly different from AI. This lays the foundations for a responsible use of gen AI at scale.

3. Redesign Workflows

Individual tasks do not exist in a vacuum. They are always part of a bigger system connected to other tasks through workflows. They often have touchpoints with tasks from other processes and teams across the organization. This suggests that generative AI's impact can extend well beyond discrete tasks and trigger a transformation of the way humans work. Redesigning processes in the age of generative AI requires a shift away from a pure technology-driven principle of offloading to machines those activities that humans previously performed. Instead, the focus should be on designing for collaboration and dialogue, where humans and AI dynamically work together.[3] You need to establish clear guidelines for human-AI workflow. Define when gen AI should seek human input and vice versa and outline how AI and humans communicate and collaborate. For example, gen AI may propose a draft plan and then seek human input to refine it, rather than making decisions on its own.

REINVENTING WORKFLOWS IN A PRODUCT DEVELOPMENT TEAM

Consider a team in the process of innovating a product line with new features. The workflow consists of a sequence of tasks, from analyzing and extracting customer insights, brainstorming new ideas, converging on a new concept, evaluating the new concept and underlying assumptions, to testing and validating for a robust business case.

Gen AI can significantly enhance the traditional workflow of various tasks in collaboration with human workers and managers. At the beginning of the workflow, gen AI acts as a Co-Pilot in analyzing large volumes of customer data to extract common patterns and identify emerging trends, with humans providing guidance on the research focus and making business sense of the insights. Based on emerging insights, gen AI can assist in brainstorming and idea generation, while human creativity guides the process by refining AI concepts to align with strategic goals and operational constraints. Then, as concepts are evaluated, gen AI supports the process with methodological guidance for thinking through the various dimensions and trade-offs.

Throughout, there is iterative collaboration and a dynamic exchange between humans and gen AI based on their strengths: AI provides analytical capabilities, breadth of ideas, different perspectives, and methodological guidance, while humans provide context, critical thinking, emotional intelligence, and domain knowledge.

Managers should also pay special attention to a variety of potential risks and regulatory pitfalls.[4] They should consider what they can and cannot do with gen AI, and they should cultivate awareness of aspects that might be extremely sensitive (for example, preventing gen AI from scrutinizing employees).

Moreover, as gen AI not only expedites tasks but also reshapes the way people work within organizations, it's imperative to reflect on its impact on human relationships. Your role is to monitor gen AI's influence on your team relationships: Does it decrease opportunities for collaboration and communication? Does it cause anxiety and uncertainty? Remind your team that they should use gen AI in a way that fosters positive and productive human relationships. For example, do not limit the use of gen AI to individual use (one-on-one settings), but include it in collaborative team brainstorming sessions (one-to-many setting).

BE AWARE OF THE POTENTIAL IMPACTS ON TEAM DYNAMICS

While the use of gen AI can enhance team performance, it's important to reflect on potential risks that may arise in team dynamics if not used appropriately.

Use this list of questions for both personal reflection and discussing with your team the impact of gen AI on their work:

- Does using gen AI individually hinder team collaboration and communication?

(Continued)

- Do team members prefer asking the machine questions rather than asking teammates?

- Has the number of group work sessions decreased markedly?

As workflows evolve, you might also need to adjust the structure of your organization or team—and that new structure might include AI chatbots and agents as well as humans. It's too early to say what direction your organizational redesign might move in, but in the past, new technologies often changed the way people worked first and then led to broader reorganizations.

4. Establish Collective Responsibility

As gen AI becomes part of the way your team works, such integration introduces a level of uncertainty and potential risks. A key difference from previous technologies is that, despite its impressive capabilities, gen AI is not infallible. A calculator is always right; gen AI is not. Given its statistical foundation, there's a risk of inaccuracy and error. Ultimately, human assessment is required to verify the quality of the output generated by LLMs.[5] The situation is further complicated by the "trust trap" (see chapter 3), which is the tendency of individuals to place too much trust in these systems.

Companies have responded to these risks in many ways. Most have taken a cautious approach—some have banned gen AI altogether. But, of course, total freedom may bring uncontrolled risks. A better solution involves a balanced approach: At the company level, leaders must emphasize trust and responsibility and create an ethical framework for fair, safe, and sustainable use of gen AI. At the individual level, users must set the appropriate context for human-AI decision-making and apply critical thinking. Managers should focus on equipping their teams with these critical skills at all levels. This sensemaking allows team members to anticipate potential risks and spot anomalies, such as catching fabrications and hallucinations.

INDIVIDUAL JUDGMENT VERSUS COLLECTIVE JUDGMENT

Individual judgment. Judgment extends beyond decision moments. It starts with framing questions accurately and considering broader contexts. In conversations with gen AI, output quality hinges on human input and feedback, which provide vital context. Judgment arises from integrated human-AI dialogue. Experimentation with gen AI demands exercising judgment before (setting clear goals), during (asking pertinent questions, providing context), and after (carefully interpreting recommendations).

Collective judgment. Teams should exercise their collective judgment by adopting collaborative practices, such as seeking validation from expert colleagues when the machine suggests ideas or solutions that fall within their domain of expertise. In addition, teams should use peer review processes in which teammates help each other review results generated by AI.

Toward a "HumanAIzed" Future for Organizations

This book not only demonstrates the integration of gen AI into management but also outlines a clear path toward what we refer to as "humanAIzed" organizations—a future where the fusion between humans and intelligent machines occurs on a large scale.[6] It is a future where an increasing number of workflows are designed for integrated collaboration between humans and AI.

Predicting the pace of organizational change is challenging, as it depends on the adoption rate and technological advancements. But one thing is certain: Companies need to prepare now for a humanAIzed future.

Standing still in the face of rapid technological evolution is no longer feasible. Expecting to win in the market with outdated tools, practices, and ways of working simply isn't an option.

It's up to managers to experiment and show what the future may look like. By moving forward with confidence and responsibility, you as a manager can pave the way for a brighter future of collaboration and innovation.

NOTES

1. Elisa Farri, Paolo Cervini, and Gabriele Rosani, "Good Judgment Is a Competitive Advantage in the Age of AI," hbr.org, September 25, 2023, https://hbr.org/2023/09/good-judgment-is-a-competitive-advantage-in-the-age-of-ai.

2. Arnaud Chevallier, Frédéric Dalsace, and Jean-Louis Barsoux, "The Art of Asking Smarter Questions," *Harvard Business Review*, May–June 2024, https://hbr.org/2024/05/the-art-of-asking-smarter-questions.

3. Paul Baier, David DeLallo, and John J. Sviokla, "Your Organization Isn't Designed to Work with GenAI," hbr.org, February 26, 2024,

https://hbr.org/2024/02/your-organization-isnt-designed-to-work
-with-genai.

4. Reid Blackman and Ingrid Vasiliu-Feltes, "The EU's AI Act
and How Companies Can Achieve Compliance," hbr.org, February 22,
2024, https://hbr.org/2024/02/the-eus-ai-act-and-how-companies
-can-achieve-compliance.

5. Peter Cappelli, Prasanna (Sonny) Tambe, and Valery Yakubov-
ich, "Will Large Language Models Really Change How Work Is Done?"
MIT Sloan Management Review, March 4, 2024, https://sloanreview
.mit.edu/article/will-large-language-models-really-change-how-work
-is-done/.

6. Harvard Business Review, *The Year in Tech 2025* (Boston, Harvard Business Review Press, 2024).

Glossary

AI agent. An autonomous system or program capable of performing tasks independently.

Artificial intelligence (AI). A term coined by Stanford professor John McCarthy in 1955 to indicate "the science and engineering of making intelligent machines." In the business context, AI is usually supported by machine learning algorithms that make progressively better decisions or predictions over time.

Co-Pilot. A mode of interaction with gen AI models in which the technology is used to facilitate task execution and enhance productivity.

Co-Thinker. A mode of interaction with gen AI models in which the technology serves as a sparring partner, fostering conversational reflection and critical thinking.

Dialogue. Structured conversation between human and machine, designed to emulate the flow of a humanlike conversation.

Fabrication. It is a type of AI hallucination. It occurs when the AI fabricates false citations or creates content from scratch that appears legitimate, but does not correspond to actual published work or research.

Generative AI (gen AI). An AI program that can learn from and mimic large amounts of data to create content such as text, images, music, videos, code, and more, based on inputs or prompts.

Generative pre-trained transformer (GPT). A type of LLM design, introduced by OpenAI, that uses a hybrid training approach, with an initial pretraining that is unsupervised and then a supervised fine-tuning phase.

Guardrails on content. Instructions included in the prompt to guide the gen AI model such as type of information and data sources to refer to; what's in scope and out of scope to avoid going off topic; what's appropriate and what is not; examples to consider as reference.

Guardrails on process. Steps and instructions included in the prompt that encompass the sequence of activities to perform; methodological approach and criteria to use; type and format of desired output.

Hallucination. An answer provided by generative AI that sounds plausible but is made up and incorrect.

Input box. The space where you type instructions, also known as the "chat window" of the gen AI model.

Large language model (LLM). An AI program with a mathematical map—across many dimensions—of the relationships among a large number of words, usually broken down into tokens.

Multi-agent system. A group of intelligent agents that interact, communicate, share information, and work together to solve a complex problem. Compared to AI chatbots, AI agents are capable of acting autonomously.

Natural language processing (NLP). A branch of AI focused on how computers can process language like humans do. Emerging business uses of NLP include speech recognition, language understanding, and language generation.

Prompt. The instruction given to a gen AI model to generate content.

Setting. Context in which the human-machine interaction takes place. It can be an individual or a group setting (for example, gen AI used in a workshop).

Synthetic data. Data that is artificially generated to mimic the characteristics and relationships inherent in real data, but without any direct link to actual events or individuals.

Index

Index

About the Authors

Elisa Farri is vice president of Capgemini Invent's Management Lab, the strategy and transformation arm of Capgemini Group.

Included in the list of management thinkers to watch by Thinkers50, Elisa is an expert on management at the intersection of academia and business. Through exploratory research, thought leadership, and academic collaborations, Elisa bridges the latest management frameworks into practice. A frequent contributor to *Harvard Business Review*, Elisa has extensive experience developing and delivering executive training at leading organizations globally. Previously, Elisa was a researcher at the Harvard Business School Research Center in Paris, France.

Gabriele Rosani is director of content and research at Capgemini Invent's Management Lab.

Esteemed author and frequent contributor to *Harvard Business Review*, Gabriele has been researching, designing, and testing new management frameworks and tools for over a decade. Gabriele works at the intersection of strategy, innovation, and sustainability, bringing new management practices to the real world of business for clients. An experienced adviser to *Fortune* 500 companies, Gabriele previously worked at the European Centre for Strategic Innovation, where he discovered his passion for shaping the new frontier of management.

About Capgemini

Capgemini is a global business and technology transformation partner, helping organizations to accelerate their dual transition to a digital and sustainable world while creating tangible impact for enterprises and society. It is a responsible and diverse group of 340,000 team members in more than 50 countries. With its strong 55-plus-year heritage, Capgemini is trusted by its clients to unlock the value of technology to address the entire breadth of their business needs. It delivers end-to-end services and solutions leveraging strengths from strategy and design to engineering, all fueled by its market-leading capabilities in AI, cloud, and data combined with its deep industry expertise and partner ecosystem.

Smart advice and inspiration from a source you trust.

If you enjoyed this book and want more comprehensive guidance on essential professional skills, turn to the HBR Guides Boxed Set. Packed with the practical advice you need to succeed, this seven-volume collection provides smart answers to your most pressing work challenges, from writing more effective emails and delivering persuasive presentations to setting priorities and managing up and across.

Harvard Business Review Guides

Available in paperback or ebook format. Plus, find downloadable tools and templates to help you get started.

- Better Business Writing
- Building Your Business Case
- Buying a Small Business
- Coaching Employees
- Delivering Effective Feedback
- Finance Basics for Managers
- Getting the Mentoring You Need
- Getting the Right Work Done

- Leading Teams
- Making Every Meeting Matter
- Managing Stress at Work
- Managing Up and Across
- Negotiating
- Office Politics
- Persuasive Presentations
- Project Management

Notes

Notes

Notes

Notes

Notes

Notes

Notes

Notes

Notes

Notes

Notes